# You Can't Leave
# & Other Stories

Lucy Staunton

Copyright © 2025 Lucy Staunton

ISBN: 9781918264791

All rights reserved, including the right to reproduce this book, or portions thereof in any form. No part of this text may be reproduced, transmitted, downloaded, decompiled, reverse engineered, or stored, in any form or introduced into any information storage and retrieval system, in any form or by any means, whether electronic or mechanical without the express written permission of the author.

This is a work of fiction. Names and characters are the product of the author's imagination and any resemblance to actual persons, living or dead, is entirely coincidental.

The views expressed in this work are solely those of the author and do not necessarily reflect the views of the publisher, and the publisher hereby disclaims any responsibility for them.

# Contents

| | |
|---|---:|
| You Can't Leave | 1 |
| Not Long Now | 62 |
| Another Time | 94 |
| You Should Have Listened | 104 |
| The Note That Changed Everything | 136 |
| Do I Know You? | 167 |

# You Can't Leave

Lifting the keys off the hook, Holly silently let herself out of the back door and ran. Not daring to look back, and having practised the route many times on her walks with Tasha, she was at the garage within minutes.

'Come on... come on...' she murmured as she put the keys in the ignition and the car began turning over. 'Please, please, please...' she whispered as it spluttered, trying desperately hard to stop the panic from taking over. On the third try, it fired up and she quickly pulled out onto the road.

Heading out in the pitch black, she kept her lights off, navigating the roads she knew so well now. Four years of running away, of being caught and put in the bunker, just for a day at first and then for longer and longer. Left hungry, dirty, desperate for it to end, only for it to start all over again until she'd 'learnt her lesson' - she'd spent the last ten months planning this day and being 'a good girl.'

As she neared the top of the hill, she knew it was only just over a mile before she'd be out on the open road and on her way back home. *Mum won't believe it when she opens the door*, she thought to herself smiling. 'I'm coming home mum,' she whispered.

Seeing the main road in the distance, she put her foot down on the accelerator.

Bang! The car stalled, coming to an abrupt stop. 'No, no, no!' she screamed, turning the key over and over, desperate for the car to start. 'You can't do this now!' she shouted, hitting her hand on the steering wheel. 'Please, come on, come on.' But it was no good.

Opening the car door, she could see that she'd stopped on a cattle grid. She then saw why the car had stopped so suddenly. Two metal poles had sprung up from the grid and were jammed under the car. *'What the hell?'*

Running as fast as she could, she could see the main road was only a hundred yards or so ahead, but it was too late. She had a welcoming party.

'You stupid girl Holly...'

'Please don't put me in the bunker again!' she pleaded as they put her in the truck.

Three hours later, and having discussed how unproductive her time with them had been, her necklace was removed and she was put with the others.

*One year later*

'Where the hell is the satnav taking us?!' exclaimed Lisa, not used to driving in the countryside.

'Definitely the scenic route!' Amy replied smiling, turning up the music as one of her favourite songs had just started playing. Singing along, with the windows down, the roads seemed to get narrower and narrower. With the high hedges cutting out any views of what was on the other side, Lisa started slowing down.

'Bloody hell!' she said, beeping around every corner until the satnav suddenly stopped working as their phones lost all signal. 'Oh, for god's sake!'

A mile or so down the road, they had both stopped talking and were instead focussed on trying to see any signs to help them. Turning another tight bend, they both spotted a white signpost tucked into the hedge. 'Thank god for that,' said Lisa, 'I could do with a drink and a quick wee!' and they followed the road down until they reached a garage with a small shop and a pub on the opposite side of the road.

Pulling into the garage, Lisa was first out, feeling quite desperate now. As she pushed open the door, a doorbell tinkled, and she was greeted by a guy in overalls. 'Can I help you?' he asked.

'Oh yes, have you got a loo? We've been on the road for ages, got a bit lost and I'm pretty desperate,' she said.

'Um - ours isn't working but you're welcome to pop over to the pub. Just tell Dave that Kev sent you over,' he replied smiling.

'Oh ok!' and she flew straight over to the pub. She had considered hopping over one of the gates into a field but hadn't found anywhere to safely pull over.

'Can I get you anything? Petrol, got a few snacks in the shop if you're hungry?' he said to Amy as he wandered out onto the forecourt and she got out of the car to stretch her legs.

'Actually, have you got any cold drinks?'

''Course, come and see what takes your fancy,' and she followed him into the garage shop.

Lisa then arrived back at her side, feeling much better. 'They do some basic pub grub over the road, all fresh produce from the farm here he says. Shall we grab a meal and a drink, and then the guy says he'll show us the way out if we want?'

'Sounds like a plan.'

'You can leave your car here if you like,' Kevin offered, and grabbing their handbags, they headed over to the pub.

'So what brings two lovely girls to this part of the world,' Dave asked smiling at them, from behind the bar.

'Uh, just a weekend away,' Lisa cut him off, looking down at the menu and rolling her eyes at Amy.

'Can I get you a drink while you're deciding?'

'Um, any chance you've got Prosecco?' Lisa answered still not looking up from the menu.

'Sorry love. We've got white wine though, if that's any good?'

'Well I'll need to see the bottle, bring it over will you?'

Arriving at their table, he presented the bottle for Lisa to see. 'Ughh.'

'That will be fine, thank you,' Amy answered smiling at him and nudging Lisa's arm, feeling a bit uncomfortable at her manner. As he left them to grab a couple of glasses, she whispered, 'Lucky we found this place, we could have been driving around for hours getting more and more lost. Be nice to him, he's seems nice enough.'

'Looks a bit inbred to me. But guess you're right and I'm bloody starving, so hope the food is good.' Arriving with their glasses, he took their orders and headed off to the kitchen.

'Do you do *everything* around here then?' Lisa called out after him. He didn't answer.

Fifteen minutes later, the first plate of gammon and chips was carefully carried out by a young girl asking if they would like any ketchup or mayonnaise. Dave walked closely behind with the second plate.

'Oh, could we have both please?' answered Amy.

'Yes,' and she skipped off to get them.

'Thank you so much - so what's your name?' Amy asked her, as she arrived back at their table.

'Tasha.'

'What a lovely name,' she replied smiling at her, as she skipped off again to see why Dave was calling her from the kitchen.

Their meal was delicious and before long, Amy was stood at the bar dinging the bell.

'Everything ok?' Dave asked, appearing from a back room.

'Really lovely thank you,' she replied, handing him some cash to settle their bill. Passing her her change, she then handed him a one pound coin back. 'This is for Tasha.'

'Thank you, that's very kind of you.' He then said he'd meet them out the front in about five minutes, so Amy popped into the loo before leaving.

Sat in his van with Tasha sat next to him, Dave wound down his window to check they were ready to go. 'See you then,' Kevin called out as Amy thanked them again for all their hospitality.

Following him through the winding roads, it was another fifteen minutes or so before they reached a B2356 sign and the satnav sprung into action. Pulling into a lay-by, Dave waved them on.

'Thank you,' they called out and were on their way.

Watching them drive off, Tasha said 'I really like the one with the dark hair. She's really nice and looks a little bit like mummy...'

A weekend of sea air, meals out and late nights followed for the next three days, before it was time to head home again.

'Right, if the satnav looks like it's taking us to the bloody middle of nowhere, we're going to ignore it this time!' announced Lisa, as she set it up to take them home.

Both feeling quite tired from their packed weekend, and neither looking forward to the week back at work, the mood was a little more subdued on the way back. Music volume on low, they chatted about how they must do this again before the year is out and other places they both fancied exploring. They also reminisced about how as work colleagues they hadn't hit it off straight away, but being tasked with making a round of redundancies in their department had kick-started their relationship. With Lisa being the more brutally honest of the two of them, and Amy having the people skills, they actually complimented each other really well. Disastrous relationships and a love of wine sealed their bond.

'Oh for fuck's sake!'
'Let's just stay on this road - I'm sure the signal will be back in a minute,' suggested Amy, as the screen had gone blank.

As the hedges began closing in on them again, Lisa suddenly stopped as she spotted a gateway on their right. Climbing the gate, she looked around desperately searching for any sign of a main road. But it was just trees and fields for miles. Getting back in, she decided the best option was to turn around. If they went back the way they came, they *had* to find the main road again and would then ask someone.

With no room to do even a ten-point turn, they both agreed to keep their eyes peeled for a space to turn around in. But half a mile later, the car suddenly veered left into a hedge.

'What the hell!!' Lisa sprung out of the door to take a look. Seeing two completely flat tyres, with large nails poking out of them, she gave the front tyre a kick and started swearing profusely, while Amy looked down, to try and stop laughing before getting out.

But it soon dawned on them that they had a problem. Neither of their phones seemed to have enough signal to phone anyone.

'We're going to have to walk and find a house with a phone we can use, aren't we?' suggested Amy.

'But what if someone hits my car?'

They both stood in silence looking around, hoping that somehow someone would miraculously appear. But after a few minutes realised a walk was their only option. Locking the doors and knowing they hadn't passed any houses for miles the way they had come, they started along the road. Within a few minutes, hearing a vehicle heading their way, they smiled at each other and instantly felt a slight sense of relief.

'You two ok?' the old man asked, quickly stopping and getting down from the tractor.

'Um, not really - got two punctured tyres,' said Lisa, pointing up the road to where they'd left her car.

'Well, I could fit your spare but that's not really going to help is it? Tell you what, there's a garage not far from here, hop in if you like and I'll take you. They've got loads of tyres in stock, bet they can help.'

'Oh thanks, but think it might be better if we wait here. Would you be able to go for us?' Lisa quickly replied, before Amy could say anything different.

'Suit yourself. I can go for you but maybe we should try and push your car to the field entrance just up here - safer to get you off the road.'

'Good idea, thanks,' smiled Lisa, feeling relieved. With Lisa steering the best she could, Amy and the old man slowly pushed the car to the grassy gateway. Thanking him again, they waved him off and stood by the car to await his return.

'Maybe we should have gone with him? Doesn't really seem fair does it?' said Amy, feeling a bit bad that he was putting himself out for complete strangers.

'We're also not stupid,' replied Lisa, smiling at her.

But as it started getting dark, they were both concerned that he hadn't returned.

'What was that?' exclaimed Amy, hearing some noises coming from beyond the gate.

'God, I don't know, probably just a fox or something. Tell you what, let's sit in the car with the doors locked.'

Sat in the front seats, keeping an eye on the wing mirrors hoping to see the old man, they were both trying to stay calm.

'Bloody hell, it's 9.30pm. He's not coming back is he?'

'Doesn't look like it,' replied Amy yawning.

'Why don't we see if we can get a bit of sleep and then at first light, we'll have to see if we can find that garage he was talking about?'

Lisa reclined her chair as far as it would go and got in as comfy a position as possible.

An hour later, Amy finally drifted off, trying to ignore the odd wildlife noises from outside, and instead getting her brain to focus on where they might book for their next break.

But nearing midnight, Lisa suddenly awoke to see some headlights lighting up the hedges nearby. Watching a car stop in the middle of the road a distance behind them, her heart began racing as its lights were switched off and she could see two people in black quietly get out and head towards their car. There wasn't enough time to get out, so pressing the central locking button again to double-check the doors were locked, she quickly nudged Amy and whispered, 'Shit! Don't panic but you need to pretend to be asleep - there's someone coming!'

As the first person approached the car, she could hear them trying each door. She could then hear another voice and watched in the wing mirror, as both people returned to their car to get something out of the boot.

'Amy we've got to get out, NOW!' she whispered in a panicked voice as she quietly lifted the central locking button. Amy silently opened her door, slid out, and grabbing hold of Lisa's hand, dragged her across the seat. Gently pushing the door to, they crawled up to the hedge and squeezed through the gap.

'Run!'

Heading for the bottom of the field, neither of them stopped running no matter how much their stitches dug into their sides. It was only as they entered the woodland at the bottom that they dared to look back, to see two figures silhouetted against the sky at the top of the field.

'What the fuck is going on here?' said Lisa panting and clutching her side.

'God knows, but I'm really worried,' Amy replied, trying to take deep breaths to calm her breathing.

Both pulled their phones out but still had no signal.

'I mean, we're in the arse end of bloody nowhere with some local frigging weirdos trying to get in our car - for fuck's sake! What are we going to do?!' exclaimed Lisa, starting to feel a sense of despair as she scanned the woods to see nothing obvious that could help them.

'I guess all we can do is keep trying our phones. Once we get some signal, we'll call the police and they can track us down.'

With only the moonlight to guide them and the rain now pouring down, they ran through the dense forest, swerving and dodging trees in their way, their faces getting scratched from the branches they didn't see in time. Panicking at every noise and twig snapping, they pulled their phones out of their pockets every few minutes, praying for a signal to appear. 'Come on, please!' Amy whispered to her phone. But nothing.

Within a short time, they could hear water. But drawing closer, they also heard voices and suddenly spotted a torchlight scanning the forest ahead. Ducking down behind a large tree, they waited as the voices grew louder.

Tugging Amy's sleeve, Lisa whispered, 'Oh god, they're coming this way. Let's head for the water,' and she took hold of her hand.

Keeping near to the ground, they made their way to a slope and quietly slid down the muddy bank to the water's edge. Seeing how fast-flowing the river was, Amy whispered, 'But what about our phones?'

'Well, they're no bloody use to us here anyway so let's try and keep them out of the water, but otherwise it's tough. Hope we find a house or a busy road - someone to help us. Shit, there are more lights now!' And seeing at least three torches scanning the top of the slope, they silently slipped into the water.

With the current taking them quickly away from the lights, they tried to stay close to each other and near the edge, grabbing hold of the odd branch to slow them down. As they were swept around a large bend in the river, glancing back, the lights had disappeared and they could finally see ahead in the moonlight.

'I'm so cold,' said Amy shivering uncontrollably. 'I can't stay in here for long; I'm not feeling so good.'

'We can't get out yet, can we? Let's try and get a bit further down. I've got you Amy,' answered Lisa, supporting her arm.

Ten minutes or so later, Amy was starting to panic as she was beginning to feel really unwell. 'Remember, I've got you, just a bit further now,' said Lisa, seeing something in the water ahead. As they neared, she could see a small jetty so guided them towards it. Bumping into one of the struts, she grasped hold of it, whilst keeping hold of Amy at the same time.

'Open your eyes Amy, we're getting out,' she told her, as she pushed Amy upwards. Finding some strength from somewhere, and with Lisa pushing her up from behind, Amy clambered up onto the wooden platform. Collapsing on her back, she lay there shivering violently before turning over and being sick all over the wooden planks at her feet.

'I'm really not well Lisa.'

'I know, I'm going to get some help. There looks to be a cottage just up from here, I'll be right back!'

With a small outside light from the cottage to guide her, she ran as fast as she could in her soaking wet clothes. Knocking on the door, she peered through the small pane of glass to see if she could see anyone, but no-one came.

'Shit, shit, shit!' and spotting the doorbell, she pressed it. Nothing. So she pressed it again and again. Still nothing.

Trying the door handle, the door creaked open.

'Hello, hello,' she called out. 'Is there anyone here?' Silence.

Moving around, she quickly began checking the rooms. Touching the kettle it was still slightly warm, so someone had to have been here recently, she thought. Taking hold of a blanket she had spotted on a chair, she headed upstairs to see if she could find anyone before returning to Amy. With a sliver of light escaping from a doorway onto the landing, she gently pushed the door open to see an old lady tucked up, fast asleep.

A nightlight gently lit the bedside table next to her, showing a glass of water and two hearing aids. Sneaking over, she gently nudged the old lady's arm. No response. Then just as she was leaving the room, she heard a startled cry.

'Who are you and what are you doing in my house?' the old lady cried out.

'It's okay. I'm not going to hurt you or anything,' said Lisa, as she rushed over to pass her her hearing aids.

As she popped them in, Lisa said, 'I really am so sorry but me and my friend are in trouble. We've broken down and there are some strange men looking for us. My friend is really poorly. Can I bring her into your house and maybe we could use your phone and get dry - would that be okay?'

'Oh my goodness, of course! Go and get her. I'll find you some fresh towels and put the kettle on. Quick, go now!'

And as the lady grabbed her dressing gown, Lisa ran out to get Amy.

Wrapping the blanket around her, she quickly got Amy to her feet and helped her up to the cottage.

With the lights now on, the old lady showed them straight into the kitchen and passed them some thick, fluffy towels. The heat from the Aga was so welcoming and cupping a hot drink in their hands, they gradually started to warm.

'You could really do with getting out of those clothes you know,' suggested the old lady.

'But we left everything in my car,' said Lisa. 'But thank you for this; it's so kind of you. It must have been so scary opening your eyes to see me at the foot of your bed!'

'Sure was!' she chuckled. 'Tell you what, I'm sure I still have some old clothes from my daughter upstairs. They might fit; shall I go and get them?'

'Thank you. Yes, if you don't mind, that would be great,' replied Lisa, while Amy had still barely spoken a word. But she seemed to be keeping her drink down, so that was a good sign she hoped.

Hearing the opening and shutting of drawers and cupboard doors upstairs, the old lady arrived back with some jumpers and trousers. They were slightly too big for them, but it was heavenly getting out of their sodden clothes.

'Pass them here, I'll put them in the tumble dryer,' the old lady said, as they quickly fished their phones out of their pockets before she took their clothes off them.

With Amy looking a little less like death, Lisa took hold of her phone. 'Miraculously, it looks ok!' she exclaimed, grinning. But then found there was still no signal. Amy's, on the other hand, had completely died.

'Doesn't matter, there's no signal here anyway. Can we use your phone?' Lisa asked, seeing Amy starting to look really upset.

''Course dear. It's on the side in the hall,' said the lady, pointing in that direction.

And whilst Amy sat at the kitchen table, Lisa went to use the phone. 'Crikey, this must be from the Antiques Roadshow,' she muttered looking at the large round dial face on the phone. 'Sorry, but how does this work?' she called out.

As the lady shuffled out of the kitchen to go and show her, Amy sat looking around the room. Something wasn't quite right. The lady being so welcoming, the clothes...

'Lisa, can you come and help me go to the loo? I don't feel so good.'

'Lisa!' she called out again, slightly alarmed after getting no response.

Then she saw Lisa in the reflection of the door's glass, and a man plunge a knife straight into her neck. Hearing her let out a small gasp as her body slumped in his arms; she then watched her being dragged towards the front door.

Rushing upstairs to the toilet, she shut herself in. Frantically looking around, she opened the medicine cabinet above the sink to find it was completely bare apart from dust, an old toothbrush and a packet of paracetamol. Turning the packet over, she gulped as she saw the expiry date, 31.08.1981. 'Oh, please no,' she whispered as she desperately tried to prise the window open. It was only a few seconds before she noticed the nails.

Silently opening the bathroom door, she crept along the small landing into each bedroom. Apart from the lady's room, every room was the same. Cobwebs and a few furnishings covered in sheets. Like no-one had lived here for a very long time. Like your worst horror film. 'This can't be happening, I'm going to wake up in a minute,' she whispered to herself.

But the lady's voice calling up the stairs reminded her of her reality.

'Everything ok dear? I've just put the kettle on again. Your friend has just been picked up to go and get some help. I'm sure she won't be long. Come and have something to eat, you must be starving.' Amy had no choice. She would have to play along for now, so made her way back down to the kitchen.

Slowly eating her toast, she had to block all thoughts of Lisa out of her mind. There was no time for that now.

'See. I knew you were hungry,' the lady smiled at her, crossing the kitchen to fetch Amy a drink. 'Now, drink this. It will make you feel better,' she said, placing the cup on the table in front of her.

'I'm not actually that thirsty, thank you though,' Amy said, not trusting what was actually in the cup.

'You must have a drink, it's important.' Taking a seat at the table next to her, the expression on the old lady's face had changed. 'Come on now, don't be silly about this.'

'Where did Lisa go?' she asked, hoping the change in subject would buy her some more time.

'I already told you - she went to get you some help with a friend of mine. They'll be back soon, don't you worry your pretty little head about anything,' was her reply.

Suddenly getting up from the table, still without taking a sip of her drink, Amy headed straight for the front door. But it was locked. 'I'm going to go and look for Lisa, please can you open this door?' she called out, making a noise pulling on the handle again and again. With the old lady not coming to her aid, she turned and ran down the hall to the back door. It was locked too.

Running in and out of each room now, trying all the windows, her chest was getting tighter as the panic properly set in. 'Why are you doing this?' she screamed out, banging on the door.

'Now there's no need to get upset dear. You're going to be absolutely fine, I promise,' said the old lady, appearing in the doorway.

Rushing past her, she heard a crackle of a radio. 'What was that?' she demanded.

Ignoring her, the old lady shuffled back into the kitchen and started busying herself, drying up a couple of plates and putting them back in the cupboard. Another crackle and Amy ran to her side. 'It sounds like a walkie-talkie or something!' and she began searching for the source. Opening and closing the few cupboard doors, she moved onto the fridge and oven. Nothing. But it was also becoming apparent and obvious, that this house was not normally lived in. *No-one lived like this.*

Another crackle. This time, it sounded like it was coming from the lounge. Lifting the cushions on the small sofa and chair, she found nothing. An old wooden bureau, with some dried-up old bottles of ink and a few sheets of paper strewn inside, and a drinks cabinet both proved fruitless. Standing still, she waited to see if she could hear it again.

The whole cottage had gone completely silent. She couldn't even hear the old lady now. *Crackle.* She ran back into the empty kitchen and then down the hall to the back door. *Crackle*, louder this time. Yanking on the door handle, it opened. Rushing out into the fresh air, she tripped and then nothing.

Intense thirst and a vile taste in her mouth were her first thoughts, as she regained consciousness. Should she open her eyes? Amy wasn't sure she wanted to see where she was. Was it all a dream - or a nightmare? Would she find that she was still at home and late for work, with an annoyed voicemail from Lisa asking why she hadn't turned up?

What was that? A gentle brush of her forehead, but who from? A light kiss on her cheek now. Gentle and warm, sweet even. And then a whisper, 'Can you hear me?' from a young voice.

Opening her eyes, blurrily scanning the room, she recognised nothing until a young face came into view. Looking down at her, a little hand reached up to wipe her tear away. 'Shall I get you a glass of water?' and before she had the chance to answer, the little face disappeared and returned quickly with a drink for her.

'Here you are,' she said smiling at her.

With no-one else seemingly in the room, she slowly sat up and took hold of the glass.

'Thank you,' she said hoarsely and then downed the whole glass.

'Are you ok? Do you remember me?' the little girl asked, hopefully.

'It's Tasha from the pub, isn't it?' Amy answered, looking at her little face.

'Yep,' and she looked truly happy to be here with Amy. 'Do you like your room?' she asked, skipping off to go and pick up the penguin cushion from the chair on the other side of the room.

Handing it to Amy, she told her that she had bought it for her especially. 'And this too!' she said excitedly, as she went to open a drawer. Pulling out a Boots No.7 bag, she skipped back to her bed. Looking inside, it was filled with make-up and perfumes. 'Do you like them?'

'They're lovely, thank you,' replied Amy, as Tasha then perched herself on the edge of the bed and took hold of Amy's hand. 'Tasha, what day is it?'

'Friday, why?'

She didn't answer, instantly panicking at how she could have lost four days.

'You'll like it here with us.'

'Sorry? Oh Tasha - I have my own home to go to.'

'But daddy says you'll stay here with me. Help look after me.'

Amy shut her eyes again and lay back on the pillow. After a few minutes, Tasha whispered in her ear that she guessed she must be tired and have fallen asleep again, so she would go back downstairs and see her later. As she heard the door click shut, she sat bolt upright looking around the room. 'What the hell?' she whispered as she found her empty suitcase from Lisa's car to the side of the chair. Creeping around the room, trying not to make a sound, she opened the wardrobe and chest of drawers to find all her belongings neatly folded or on hangers. 'Jesus Christ,' she muttered, the panic rising in her chest. Slowly pulling back one of the curtains, she had to see where she was. A patchwork of fields, with cows and sheep and a couple of horses were all she could see for miles. And then something suddenly diverted her eyes elsewhere - the old lady and Kevin from the garage were looking up at her from the yard below, smiling.

Hours later, a small knock at the door and Tasha's little face peeking around it as it creaked open. 'Tea's ready! It's Nanny's roast dinner - you must be *so* hungry.'

And feeling like her stomach was caving in with hunger, she really needed some food. Slowly getting up from the bed, Tasha took hold of her hand. 'Come on!'

Showing her to the large table in the kitchen, the old lady arrived at the table with a plate piled high with roast chicken and all the trimmings. 'It's going to be ok Amy, you'll see,' she said smiling at her, and tapping her reassuringly on her shoulder.

Tasha was so excited to sit next to her and couldn't stop smiling at Amy, and touching her arm as they tucked into their meal. 'It's yummy, isn't it?'

'Yes it is,' were the only words Amy spoke at the table.

But now feeling stronger, having eaten and drunk well, her energy surged. And so did her need to get out of here. *Were they waiting for her to go nuts before saying anything?* Everyone acting and carrying on like everything was normal, chatting about their days and what they were planning to do the next day too. No-one saying a word about the extra person sat at their table.

'Why am I here?' she suddenly blurted out.

'Don't you remember dear?' the old lady piped up.

And with that, Dave from the pub arrived and took a seat with them. The old lady grabbed his plate from the oven and passed it to him. Again, he tucked in, chatting about the problems with his tractor on the farm that day and not a word about Amy sat with them. 'Where's dad?' asked Tasha.

'Oh, he's still out on the farm. He'll be back in a bit,' replied Dave.

'Dad - who's your dad Tasha?'

'Kev,' answered Dave before Tasha swallowed enough of her food to be able to answer.

'What the hell is going on?' she exclaimed, standing up at the table. 'Is no-one going to tell me why I'm here?! What is wrong with you? Stop pretending that abducting someone is normal, because it bloody well isn't!'

Everyone just looked at her.

'What does *adducted* mean?' asked Tasha.

'Right, who wants pudding?' Dave interjected, getting up from the table and starting to take their plates. 'It's Nanny's special rice pudding!'

*You Can't Leave*

'Me please! You're going to really love it Amy,' answered Tasha excitedly and got up to help Dave.

'I'll talk to you later - once Tasha's in bed,' the old lady told her with a stern look.

Amy nodded and sat back down.

An hour later, having sat and read a story to Tasha as she had pleaded with Amy that it must be her turn tonight, she tucked her up as fast as she could, desperate to have her talk.

'Promise me, you won't go,' whispered Tasha as she switched off her light. 'Promise you'll have breakfast with me in the morning, *please.*'

'Ok, I'll try,' she said, as she knew deep down that there was no way she would be staying.

The old lady was waiting at the bottom of the stairs and asked her to take a seat in the lounge.

In the dimly lit room, Amy waited for her to arrive. Passing her a cup of tea, the old lady said, 'All we want is for you to stay here for a short while and spend some time with Tasha. She misses her mum desperately and really needs to spend some time with a younger female - I'm getting on a bit now. When she saw you in the pub, you reminded her so much of her mum that we promised her you would come and stay with us for a while.'

'But you can't do this. I mean for god's sake, I've got my own life. Find someone for her yourselves! Get Kevin to find a girlfriend or something. You can't go around just taking people against their will!'

'But we can and you are here now. All you need to do is play your part. Spend time with Tasha and then after her birthday, in a little over a month, you can leave.'

'You'll let me go home in a month's time?'

'Most probably, yes. But as long as you don't try and leave beforehand, and we all give Tasha a nice birthday. It's the least she deserves.'

'No. *Probably* is no good, I have to know for sure.'

'Well, I can't promise but let's see how the month and her birthday goes. If things go ok, I'll see what I can do,' and she got up and left the room.

Wandering out into the hall, she could see the old lady had gone back into the kitchen and was now talking with Kevin.

Heading up the stairs to her room, she quietly closed her bedroom door and sat on her bed. Trying to control her breathing, she *had* to find a way out. About an hour later, hearing the old lady whisper goodnight at her door and turn off the landing light, she waited for the house to go completely silent before getting up. Carefully lifting the door latch, she crept out onto the landing and began making her way down the stairs; her heart racing at every creak. Tiptoeing through the hallway to the front door, she gently pulled on the handle. Locked. Making her way back down the hall she tried the back door, locked. The kitchen window, locked. Every room the same, windows and doors locked. Searching now for keys, they *had* to be somewhere. For a brief moment she thought about smashing the glass, but knew that wouldn't do her any good – they'd definitely hear it and find her before she'd found a way out, especially as she had no idea where she actually was. Having checked all the hooks in the hall, she crept into the lounge. Spotting a wooden bureau, she tiptoed across the room and gently lifted the lid.

'What are you doing?'

'What?!' she gasped, turning to see Kevin sat in the chair. 'Um, just needed to get a drink.'

'Well, you know where the kitchen is Amy, don't be stupid now... I thought mum spoke to you.'

Following her into the kitchen in silence, he watched her get a glass of water and go back upstairs to her room. She then heard her bedroom door being locked, from the outside.

Lying in bed, she finally let a few tears fall. Up until now, she'd had to focus purely on not ending up like Lisa, but now the reality of her situation was beginning to sink in. She was in the middle of bloody nowhere, with a weird family. Why hadn't anyone come looking for her? She must have been reported missing by now, Lisa too. And how did they end up here? They'd followed the signs, surely like everyone else driving in these parts, so where *was* everyone else? Trying not to get upset, it suddenly dawned on her that her only way out was Tasha. If she liked Amy, and she reminded her of her mum, then getting her to trust her should be easy. Then she could help her leave, just without knowing it. And that plan meant that, for now, she must play along with them, well... as long as it didn't involve anything more than being a companion for Tasha.

A little knock at her bedroom door the following morning, woke her. Tasha's little face appeared, letting her know breakfast would be ready in ten minutes. Splashing some water on her face and tying her hair up, she got dressed and arrived just as the bacon sandwiches were being handed out. 'Ketchup or brown sauce?'

'Oh, ketchup please. Thank you Tasha.'

Grinning at Amy, Tasha carefully took the lid off her sandwich, covered the bacon in ketchup, and handed it to her. It was more than she would have put on, but it was very cute of her and she looked pleased as punch with herself.

'After breakfast, do you want to come and collect the eggs with me?'

'I'd love to,' replied Amy. 'Maybe you could show me around?'

''Course I can,' said Tasha excitedly, with ketchup now covering most of her mouth.

After finishing breakfast, they quickly found Amy some wellies. 'Right you two. Here you go,' said the old lady, handing them a wicker basket lined with a tea towel for collecting the eggs. 'And you must call me Joan, ok Amy?'

'Ok.'

Trudging in their wellies across the field to the hay barns, Tasha had so many questions for Amy. Happily answering where she lived before staying with them, how old she was, whether she has a mum and dad and why she hasn't got any children of her own, Tasha skipped along while Amy carried the basket. Arriving at the hay barns, they then spent the next half an hour forgetting about the outside world, and instead chasing each other up and over the hay bales and collecting as many eggs as they could find. And caught up in all the giggling, Amy dropped pertinent questions into their play.

'So where's your mummy then?'

'She's gone.'

'Oh, where did she go?'

'Dunno.' And looking at Amy, she added, 'Are you going to leave like the other girls?'

'Sorry? What do you mean... the other girls?

'Oh, you're not the first to come and stay.'

'So where did they go?'

'Dunno... they didn't even say goodbye. So Nanny says I should stay with her, she'll always be here.'

And after a few minutes Amy asked, 'So, do you go to school?'

'Nope... Nanny says she'll learn me everything. My sister lives up the road on the other farm.'

Amy tried to show no concern on her face, like they were just having a normal conversation.

'Oh, you have a sister - so what's her name then?'

'Charlotte.'

'And is she older than you?'

'No, she's only five. We get to have sleepovers together sometimes – it's really fun. Would you like to see her?'

'Oh yes, that would be lovely.'

'We'll have to check with Nanny first though, or dad.'

'Or we could just go now? Take them some of our eggs. Is it up this way?' asked Amy, spotting a small track to the side of the field.

'Uh no, I'm not allowed to go on my own.'

'But you're not on your own, I'm with you,' Amy said smiling and taking hold of her hand.

'Ok then. I think it's up this way,' and they began following the small path.

But the sign ahead suddenly sank all hope Amy had. The field and gate were protected with electric fences, with a large warning sign alerting them to the danger. 'Have you ever touched them accidentally?' asked Amy, pointing at the wires around the perimeter of the field.

'Yeah, *ooh* it hurted so much. I cried for ages, until Nanny got a bit cross.'

'Maybe they're not on today,' Amy said hopefully. 'Let me find something to test it, shall I?'

'No don't. They're always on, especially when we have visitors.'

'But they're supposed to be for keeping the animals in, aren't they? So they don't escape. And the field is empty.'

'Well, *you* can try if you like?'

Picking up a stick lying in the grass, Amy wandered over to the perimeter and poked it. Nothing. Holding the stick on it, again nothing. 'Maybe they're not on today after all?' she said, as she touched it with the end of her index finger. Intense pain, as the electricity surged up through her hand, made her recoil and Amy knew then that it was no good.

'Are you alright? See, we'll have to ask Nanny or dad.'

Holding and rubbing her hand, they then heard a tractor making its way up the field. 'It's dad!' Tasha called out and went running towards it.

'Amy's hurted herself,' she said as Kevin pulled up.

'Can she not read?' said Kevin loudly, getting out and walking up to Amy. 'You ok?' he said, looking at her.

'Yes, fine thank you.'

'You a bit daft or summat? That's a bloody big sign we put up to warn about the fences. Come on, I'll give you a lift back to the house.' They both climbed up and took a seat in the trailer, as the tractor chugged back down to the house. Keeping a tight hold of the basket of eggs, Tasha giggled that they would 'splat everywhere' otherwise. Amy just smiled and went quiet.

After getting back and washing their wellies at the outside tap, they walked in their socks back into the kitchen. Placing the basket on the table, Tasha zoomed off to go to the loo whilst Joan stared at Amy. 'That was silly, wasn't it?'

'What?'

'Don't think that we're stupid. That was your first real test, young lady... to see if we could trust you not to try and leave straight away. I did ask you for a month, didn't I?'

Amy just looked down at the floor.

'Anyway, go and have a bit of time in your room, and we'll call you when it's time for tea,' Joan told her and she headed back upstairs.

So many thoughts were running through Amy's head as she lay on her bed. *How the hell did Kevin arrive so quickly and know she had touched the wire? It was like they had been watching her, but how could they? There's nothing here. I mean, they don't even have mobile phones or anything. The TV is even black and white, for god's sake. So it must have just been coincidence that he was in the field... yes, must have been.* But it made her feel terribly uneasy about the whole situation. *In a month's time, will they really let me go? Especially knowing she would tell the outside world about what happened to Lisa. Come to think of it, why has no-one mentioned her since the cottage? Let's see what they have to say about it over tea.*

Hearing her name being called, she quickly went to the loo and then joined them at the large table in the kitchen.

'Mmmm, it smells lovely doesn't it? I'm starving Nanny,' said Tasha, with her knife and fork ready in her hands to tuck in. Plates of cottage pie and vegetables were placed in front of them and a jug of steaming hot gravy was handed around. Everyone was quiet while they ate their food. Cutlery and plates were then collected by Kevin, ready to hand out their pudding.

'Does anyone know what happened to my friend Lisa?' Amy blurted out, breaking the silence.

'Who's Lisa?' asked Tasha.

'The lady I was sat with, the first time I met you in Dave's pub. Do you remember her Tasha?' answered Amy.

'Oh yes. You're much nicer than her,' replied Tasha, taking hold of her spoon and scooping a big mouthful of crumble and custard into her mouth.

'Um. Like I told you before, she went to get help. Maybe she couldn't find her way back again? These roads are easy to get lost in, as you know,' replied Joan.

'But she would have called the police to help her. I don't think she ever left to get help, did she? I don't think she could... not having been stabbed in the neck!'

As Tasha's face turned in horror at what she'd just heard, Kevin snapped at Amy. 'That's enough stories thank you. Ignore her Tasha, she doesn't know what she's talking about. Fancy trying to scare an eight year old girl, with silly comments like that! Tasha, listen to me. Her friend left her here and she is making stuff up, so she doesn't have to admit that maybe her friend not returning is because she isn't really a good friend after all.'

'I don't want anyone else to say a word now. Let's finish our pudding and then I need to have a chat with you Amy,' he said glaring at her.

The room went completely silent, apart from the odd scrape of their spoons on their pudding bowls. Kevin got up, taking hold of their empty bowls and stacked them in the sink. Returning with a round of drinks, he handed them out, telling them it was to celebrate being together. They clinked their glasses and he watched Amy not touch hers. 'Drink up everyone. You too Amy,' and with Tasha clinking her glass again, she smiled and drank her glass of wine. When everyone had finished, Joan announced, 'Bathtime for you Tasha,' and taking hold of her hand they left the room.

With just Amy and Kevin sat at the table now, he said quietly, 'I thought Joan explained everything, Amy. Stay for Tasha's birthday and don't try anything stupid, and then you should be able to go.'

'*Should* isn't any good to me Kevin - I have to have certainty. And I also need to know what happened to Lisa. What did you do with her?' she demanded, suddenly starting to feel the effects of the wine.

Kevin said nothing, he just waited. Ten minutes later they quietly left the house.

The following morning, Amy wasn't at breakfast. Sneaking into her room, Tasha found her bed made and no Amy.

'Where's Amy, Nanny?' she asked, taking her seat at the table.

'Oh, um, she's going to be helping out on the other farm for a little while.'

'Can I go over to the other farm and help too, then?'

'Not for now, you've got some school work here today and I need you to help me. She'll be back in a few days.'

In the damp, dark room, Amy scraped her way around the walls desperately searching for a way out. Waking up, to find that she was all alone, in the pitch black, in complete silence was terrifying. She remembered being at the table in the kitchen and then nothing. She was mad at herself for saying anything about Lisa, her thoughts now racing with the rising panic. *If only she had kept gob shut - and she definitely shouldn't have had that drink! Now, things were looking really bad. Would she ever get out? Maybe she would end up here forever.* Aloud, she snapped herself out of it, saying 'Think Amy. For god's sake, think!' But after what seemed like forever, she slumped down on what felt like an old mattress in despair. The room stank and everywhere was wet and cold. Moss seemed to cover much of the walls, but the smell was something else. *Dead rat?* she wondered. *They wouldn't leave her here, would they?* Her stomach rumbling was the only sound to break the silence. Busting for the loo now as well, she crawled around the room on her hands and knees, trying to find the bucket she'd knocked over earlier. Pulling her trousers and pants down, she tried desperately hard not to miss.

Listening out for any sounds, there was nothing... not even birds singing. And with no light, she couldn't gauge whether it was day or night. *Where the hell was she? Underground somewhere?* With no other option, she started banging on the walls and screaming for help. Clawing at anything that felt loose, she screamed louder and louder, but still no-one came and there was no way out.

Exhausted and feeling light-headed from the lack of food and drink, she eventually gave up and fell asleep on the dirty, old mattress. Two nights later, and having watched her distress, they decided that maybe she had learnt her lesson. Maybe she would behave herself now. Carefully placing a small tray with a drink and sandwich on the floor, the wall slid back into place without Amy even stirring. Keeping an eye on the screen, it was only an hour or so later, that Amy awoke to find the small tray. Shovelling the sandwich in her mouth, she then downed the glass of juice and took a deep breath. Wiping her hand across her mouth, she then began calling for someone to help her. 'Please don't leave me here,' she said with eyes filled with tears. But then she started to feel unsteady. 'I don't feel very well, please someone... help me!' and as the room began moving, she staggered back onto the mattress. And then her eyes closed.

As Amy came around again, she could sense something different. The dank, rotten smells had gone and as she opened her eyes found herself back in her bedroom. Sitting bolt upright, she ripped the duvet back and leapt out of her bed. Expecting her door to be locked, she was surprised it opened and so she headed straight for the bathroom. Glancing in the mirror, she looked awful. So after going to the loo, she jumped in the shower and then headed straight back to her room. The realisation of how things could have turned out, hit her hard. They could have left her in that bunker forever and no-one would have found her, she was sure of that. So she would have to cooperate with their crazy plan. Spend time with Tasha, be nice to her and them, and then after her birthday, somehow get the hell out of there. Surely by then, her family or the police would have come and found her.

After getting dressed, she nervously made her way downstairs to the kitchen.

'Tea?' Joan asked as she appeared.

'Yes, please.'

'Take a seat - then we can have a quick chat too,' and Joan turned back to the cupboards to grab their cups and put the kettle on.

Setting their cups down on the table, she passed Amy a slice of cake.

'No thank you,' she said looking down.

'Tasha made it, so please try some.'

Whilst she sipped her tea and nibbled her cake, Joan told her that Tasha thinks she has been spending a few days at the other farm - that was the explanation they had given as to Amy's absence. 'Don't spoil it by saying anything else, ok?'

'Yes, fine. But what if she asks me about something up there? I won't know what to say.'

'Yes we've thought of that. Kev is on his way over now and is going to take you up there. You can meet everyone and have a quick tour. Ok?'

She nodded as Kevin appeared in the doorway.

'Ready? You'll need wellies – it's been raining all morning,' and he left again.

Swapping her shoes for wellies at the back door, she then found Kevin waiting for her out the front in the tractor.

They both sat in silence, as they made their way up the field and through the open gates to the farm in the distance. As they neared, she could see it was a much larger plot than Joan and Kevin's.

'Behave yourself, ok young lady?'

She just nodded looking down at the floor.

Everyone was very friendly and welcoming, introducing her to the family and Tasha's little sister Charlotte. She had to be honest, she was shocked - they looked nothing alike. But she was very sweet, just like Tasha, and was also very excited to help show her around.

Holding her hand, she skipped along, telling her how Tasha had told her about how lovely she was. 'She's got you a present,' she suddenly blurted out, followed by 'oops, I'm not to tell you. Oh no!'

'Don't worry, I won't say anything,' Amy said smiling at her and squeezing her hand. And the little piglets in the pen ahead of them instantly stopped that conversation.

'This one's mine,' Charlotte said, running after one of them giggling and trying to catch it.

After her tour, Dave, his wife Janet, and their older son Mark joined them, with bottles of milk to help with feeding. Handing them out, they each took a seat on the surrounding hay bales and fed their eager little piglets. For a short time, Amy tried to focus all her thoughts on this moment, with Charlotte covered in mud having face-planted the floor running after her piglet, instead of the dire situation she was really in. Then hearing her name being called out, Amy turned to see Tasha waving madly at her. Running into the pen, she raced over to Amy, sitting as close as she could to her without actually being on her lap.

*You Can't Leave*

'I've missed you,' she said looking up at her.

'It's lovely to see you too,' Amy replied smiling down at her. With Tasha's head nestled into her side, she put her arm around her as the piglets took off at speed again, having now been fed. Tasha then started telling Amy about everything she'd been learning with Nanny today and how much she hated maths and times tables.

'But once you've learnt them, that's it - you'll never forget them!' Amy said reassuringly.

'Can *you* help me learn them?'

'Yes of course.'

'I've got you a surprise too! Wait 'til we get home!'

The minute Kevin stopped the tractor and they could get off, Tasha raced inside, appearing moments later with a package for her.

'What's this for?' Amy asked.

'Because you're lovely! Come on, open it!' she answered excitedly.

Inside was a silver necklace with a beautiful ornate locket. She carefully opened it to find a silver disc with a love heart painted on it. 'I drew that, *especially* for you. Will you always wear it and think of me.'

'It's beautiful Tasha, yes of course,' she replied, opening the clasp and putting it around her neck. 'Thank you,' she said smiling.

From that night onwards, Amy was in charge of times tables practice before tea and bedtime story reading. With only two weeks before Tasha's birthday, Amy made every effort to give them no reason to not let her go. Helping on the farm and with Tasha's school work, she got stuck in to pass the time as quickly as possible.

## You Can't Leave

Reading Tasha her bedtime story one night, as it came to an end and Amy got up off the bed to put it back on the bookcase, Tasha said, 'You won't go, will you?'

'Why do you say that?' Amy asked, not really wanting to answer.

'Well, mummies leave don't they?'

'I'm not sure about that.'

'I am.'

Tucking her in, she turned off the light and as she reached the door whispered, 'Good night Tasha.'

And Joan was stood there, listening and waiting for her. 'Everything ok?'

'Yes, of course,' Amy said, and squeezed past her to get to her bedroom.

Lying in bed that night, her mind was racing. A conversation she'd overheard two nights before, didn't sound like they had any plans for her to leave. Tasha apparently loved having her around - just like her mum had been returned to her. And they hadn't found anyone better yet? What??? Panic had instantly set in. She *had* to come up with a plan.

The following morning, she thought her prayers had been answered.

Sat at breakfast, the silence was interrupted by a loud whirring sound. 'What's that noise Nanny?'

Dashing across to the window, Joan answered, 'Just a helicopter going over.'

Amy leapt up from the table and ran out the back door to the yard. Shouting at the helicopter and frantically waving her arms, she watched as it neared the end of the field before beginning to turn. 'It's coming for me,' she muttered to herself, as she began running towards it, calling out even louder now. But unbeknown to her, the pilot had just received an alert about an accident, diverting the helicopter's attention to the opposite direction. And as she watched it turn and move away, she dropped to the floor in tears.

'Why are you crying?' Tasha said, arriving at her side and putting her small arm around her shoulders.

'Oh, it's nothing really. Just me being silly,' and wiping her arm across her eyes, she took hold of Tasha's hand to go back to breakfast.

She didn't need to ask what Joan was thinking, it was written all over her face. It was only fortunate that Tasha's birthday was so close now, so they'd decided just to keep her under lock and key until then.

Tasha's birthday treat was a big family meal at Dave's pub. It was the first time she'd been back there since her visit with Lisa, and oh, how she wished things had taken a different course. If only it hadn't been for the bloody satnav this might never have happened. But she couldn't let those thoughts get in the way now. She could think about that later, when she was out.

What she hadn't really noticed before was a small row of cottages they must have passed on their way down to the garage and pub. Her mind began racing.

Tasha had a lovely time, getting all the fuss being the birthday girl. And whilst all the attention and merriment was a great distraction, she was already thinking about how she could get to the cottages to see if there was a phone or anyone that could help. And maybe a game of Tasha's favourite could be the answer.

'Fancy a game of hide and seek, with *all* of us?!' she whispered in her ear, whilst everyone was chatting about getting another round of drinks. With the meal and other party games finished, now seemed like the perfect time.

'Oh heck, all of us - yeah, that would be brilliant! Yes!! Hey everyone, can we all play a game of hide and seek, *please*?!' Tasha announced.

With everyone saying 'why not,' and suggesting they finish their drinks first, it was just time to choose the hiders and the seekers.

With the split agreed, Tasha ran out the door giggling and reminding Amy that she needed to count to 100. And under the guise of searching, whilst the other seekers headed for the garage and further down the road, she split off and discreetly made her way up to the cottages. Peering in through the windows, she could see that most were unoccupied and found their doors were locked. But in the third one, she was sure she could hear a radio playing. Lightly tapping on the door, an old man appeared.

'Hello.'

'Um, oh hello. Sorry to bother you, but could I use your phone?' she asked quietly, spotting it just behind him in the hall.

'Sure,' and he left her to make her call.

'Police please, you have to help me!' she said urgently.

'What's your address?' the dispatcher asked.

'Sorry, wait a sec. What's this address?' Amy asked the old man, and relaying it she was told to wait with him and they would be there as soon as they can. 'Please hurry,' she pleaded.

Taking a seat in the lounge, the old man offered her a drink. 'No thank you, do you think they'll be long?' she asked him.

'Wouldn't have thought so,' he said reassuringly.

In the pub, Dave had just taken a phone call. Rushing downstairs, he quickly changed and got in the car waiting outside.

Hearing a knock on the door, as the old man got up to answer it Amy hurried past him. With the police officer asking her to come and get in the car, she began catching him up on everything that had happened, barely taking a breath. But as the car doors closed, the other officer sat in the front of the car turned to look at her.

'Time to take you back, Amy!' said Dave.

Frantically pulling at the car door handle to find it was child locked, Amy screamed, 'I'm in a fucking nightmare - you know I don't care anymore! Do what you want!'

Locked in a different bedroom back at the farm, they kept a close eye on her. Meals and drinks were put just inside the door, before it was quickly closed again. With an en-suite bathroom, she had no need to leave the room. And having broken their trust again, they would let her dwell on things for longer this time - just in more comfort. It was only as she started being sick that they had to let someone else in to see her.

'Amy, the doctor is here to see you.'

Entering her room, she looked like she'd given up. With the doctor doing all the basic health checks in silence, she then lay back down on the bed while he analysed the results.

'Think some fresh air out on the farm would be the best medicine for you Amy,' he said a few minutes later.

'So do you know what's wrong with me then?'

'There's nothing actually wrong with you Amy, this is why you are being sick,' and he passed her the pregnancy test stick.

Her world suddenly got a lot darker. 'But how can this be?' she whispered, staring down at the stick.

'Well, I believe you had been on a weekend away before getting here, hadn't you?'

'And I didn't sleep with anyone, so both you and I know that can't be the frigging answer, don't we! It will be one of these lot, while I was blacked out in that awful bunker! Oh my god, I can't do this!' she screamed at him.

'You can do this Amy, and you must. I'll keep an eye on you and look after you while you are here. And maybe afterwards, I'll see what I can do about you leaving.'

'No!' she shouted at him, and began hysterically pacing around the room. Grabbing a bag, she began opening drawers and shoving clothes inside. 'Get away from me!' she screamed, as the doctor tried to take the bag from her. Running into the en-suite, she needed to find something hard to smash the bedroom window. She was leaving, no matter what. But arriving back in the room with a plant pot in hand, Kevin was stood there waiting. Grabbing hold of her, he held her tightly while the needle pierced her skin and the doctor administered the sedation, only releasing his grip as she finally slumped in his arms.

Placing her back in the bed, Kevin then thanked the doctor for confirming everything, and locking the door they made their way downstairs to share the good news with everyone.

The following weeks felt like a blur for Amy. Coming round to have something to eat and drink, and go to the loo, before falling asleep again. In her drugged state, she remembered Joan talking quietly to her as she shovelled down some food and drink, and then helping her to the loo before popping her back to bed, telling her that it was important for her to rest. She thought she saw Tasha being shooed out of the room a couple of times, but it could have been a dream.

When she was finally allowed to wake properly, looking around the room her heart sank at the realisation that this was it - her situation was dire, she had no idea even what day it was. The clock said 2.30pm, but how long had she been in her room? After getting washed and dressed, and finding her bedroom door locked, she knocked loudly whilst calling out for someone to help her. Joan arrived almost immediately, like she had been watching somehow. 'Come on now, Tasha is desperate to see you Amy, my love.'

And there was Tasha's face smiling up at her, from the bottom of the stairs. Eagerly taking hold of Amy's hand, she led her to the kitchen table. Patting the seat next to her, Amy sat down next to Tasha. As Joan handed them their plates of food, Tasha began telling her about everything she had missed while she was resting: baby goats that had been born, how dad had let her steer the tractor because she'd got her six times table right, how she needed her help with eights though as they were still making her a bit cross, and how she'd missed Amy reading her bedtime stories. So the next day, Amy began catching up on everything she had missed.

For the duration of the pregnancy, she was never left alone. Apart from when she was locked in her room each night, they were always there, taking care of her, fussing her, calling the doctor any time they thought she looked like something was up. But after the initial sickness, she sailed through the pregnancy and finally unable to hide her growing bump, they had broken the news to Tasha. 'Oooh, I hope it's a boy... I would love a little brother...' she exclaimed excitedly, hopping around the kitchen. Cuddling Amy, and very gently placing her hand on her tummy, she whispered, 'I can't wait to see you and be your big sister. I will help look after you.'

But for Amy, life was a nightmare. How had nobody come to find her? She'd been missing now for months and apart from the helicopter, there had been no sign of anyone searching for her. How could this be? The place should be flooded with police cars looking for her and Lisa, surely?

While her belly grew, she focussed on Tasha, the farm and anything that was a distraction. Yes they looked after her really well, yes they did everything for her but deep down she hoped there would be something wrong and she would have to be admitted to hospital. 'Yes, maybe when she went into labour they would *have* to take her to hospital,' she thought to herself, 'so just bide your time, not long now...' But later doubled over in pain, with the worst cramps she had ever experienced, the doctor arrived by her side within minutes. And adding to her distress, she then learned that he always delivered their babies at home. All the kit had been set up in another bedroom ready, so she was just helped onto the bed in there, ready for any assistance she needed. Pain relief was administered and while Kevin kept Tasha well out of the way, Joan rubbed her back, held her hand, mopped her brow, reassuring her that she could do it. And as little Joe arrived into the world, there were cries and tears of joy. Placing the little boy on her chest, and covering him with a blanket, Amy just looked at them all. Feeling exhausted and emotional, she let a couple of tears trickle down her cheeks.

'Well done Amy, my love,' said Joan.

'Absolutely, you made my job so easy Amy,' the doctor told her, smiling.

She couldn't answer. She wanted to scream at them, that this should never have happened. But she had to be cleverer than that, she knew that now. And with little Joe starting to cry, she looked down at him wondering what the hell she was supposed to do. 'Do you want to try and breastfeed?'

'No.'

So she was passed a bottle of formula milk, already made up. Popping the teat in his mouth, he guzzled for a few seconds before falling asleep. Passing him over to Joan, she left them to go to the loo. Looking in the mirror, she rubbed her eyes, still in shock that she had just delivered a baby. A light knock at the door and she could hear Joan. 'Amy love, I'll just go and run you a bath ok.'

Hearing that it was ready for her, she slowly walked into the family bathroom and stepped into the beautifully warm bath. Sinking below the suds, she stayed under the water for a few seconds before surfacing and lying still. Half an hour later, with her hair soaking wet, she dripped her way back to the bedroom. In the short time she had been in there, her room had been lit with candles and soft music was playing. Joe was bundled up in a blanket, sleeping soundly in his Moses basket and Joan was sat waiting.

'Let me know when you are ready for visitors, Tasha is obviously desperate to come and see you and her new brother.'

'Just let me dry my hair and put some clean clothes on.'

An hour later, Tasha arrived with a sandwich she had made especially for her and a small bunch of flowers she had picked from the garden. She was so gentle and sweet, quietly creeping up to the Moses basket, and kissing Joe on the forehead. 'I love you already,' she whispered to him, which made Amy well up. It wasn't Tasha's fault that she was part of this weird family and she is such a sweet girl, she thought to herself. Tasha then sat on her bed next to her, asking her if she was ok.

'Bit tired but I'm fine thanks.' She definitely wasn't going to be sharing anything else she was feeling, mentally or physically.

With regular checks on her and Joe from the doctor, three months later they were finally allowed to go for a stroll outside in the fresh air. Tasha had been ready from 6.00am to give them a guided tour and an update on all the things that had been happening, while they had been stuck indoors.

'We've got more piglets too! Come see!' and she held onto the side of the pram to help Amy push her little brother.

'Not too close though Tasha. You don't want your brother to get poorly,' Joan called out after them.

As they neared the new additions to the farm, Tasha called out, 'You wait here with Joe. I can show you from here, ok!' and she ran off to start a running commentary. Amy smiled, as Tasha relayed all the changes to her and little Joe, even though for a change he was fast asleep.

And sadly for Amy, with no time to herself or opportunity to change things, and no-one coming to find her, she found herself staying at the farm. Neither Joan nor the doctor honoured their words to help her leave, instead admiring how well she had fitted into life there and how it had benefitted Tasha immensely. It was only in the early hours, while she was up with Joe feeding or trying to settle him with his teething pain, that she would let the tears flow.

And it was only as he neared his first birthday, that things took an unexpected turn.

The previous day, she had been handed the Argos catalogue to choose some items for Joe's birthday. After her previous attempts to leave, she'd been told in no uncertain terms that there would be serious consequences if she tried it again. *'It was her own fault that they couldn't trust her to keep her word, so she would have to remain at the farm at all times.'* And apart from one trip to the garage with Kevin and Tasha in the tractor, they had kept their word. She had never been off the premises.

With Tasha super-excited at going shopping with Joan to get Joe some birthday presents, she was tasked with keeping an eye on things at the farm.

'This is definitely the one you want?' Tasha checked with her for about the fifth time, pointing at the page in the catalogue. 'I don't want to get the wrong one!'

'Yes Tasha, I think he'll love it, don't you?!'

'Yep... come on Nanny, aren't you ready yet?'

'Alright, alright, I'm coming,' exclaimed Joan, arriving at the bottom of the stairs.

Putting their coats on, with the clouds darkening overhead, they raced out to the car. As Joan started the engine, Tasha suddenly arrived back in the house, charging through the hallway, and through the kitchen to the back door.

'Nanny thinks we need our brollies!' she told Amy, as she grabbed them out of the holder in the corner. Rushing, the holder fell on its side and everything in it landed on the kitchen floor.

'Don't worry Tasha, I'll sort that out - you get going!'

'Thanks,' she answered as she ran back out the front door and was gone. Hearing them leave, and with Joe happily crawling around on the kitchen floor, Amy put the kettle on and cleared the floor of brollies, shoe horns and odd bits that had been dumped in the holder. Popping them back in place, she then tidied up the kitchen, made a start on the casserole for tea and then sat with her cup of tea to watch Joe explore. It was so rare that they had the place to themselves; the peace and quiet of it just being the two of them was very welcome.

He seemed to find opening and closing the cupboard doors very funny. Reaching the saucepan cupboard, he giggled as he began dragging the pans out onto the floor. Spotting the space he had now made, Joe crawled off at speed into the cupboard to investigate. But hitting his head at the back he burst into tears, and as Amy leant in to drag him out he flung his arms out, hitting a small switch tucked away from view. 'What the bloody hell is that?' she muttered, hearing a noise.

Quickly turning to see where it was coming from, it sounded like it was in the broom cupboard. Picking Joe up, she carried him in with her to investigate.

'Oh my god!' she exclaimed aloud, as the inside wall had clicked open to reveal a small room hidden deep inside. A room filled with screens and more technology than she probably ever seen. 'What the...!' she muttered as they moved inside. With Joe on her hip, wriggling to get down, she could see some of the screens gave her a picture of everything that was happening there, right now: the garage, with Kevin standing beside a car chatting to Dave; the farm up the road with Charlotte cycling around the yard while Janet was pinning out some washing; the row of cottages looking completely empty; the farm here with Joan's car missing and just the animals moving around their areas of the yard. But some were blank, like they were turned off. For somewhere seemingly so off the beaten track, with no mobile signal or obvious signs of modernisation, this was all such a shock. But it also explained how they always seemed to know where she was and what she was doing. Spotting a bank of switches on the far wall, she was just about to take a closer look when she suddenly saw movement on the farm screen, alerting her that Tasha and Joan were on their way back. Rushing back out of the room, she was in a panic. Pressing the switch again, the wall took just a few seconds to click shut as she flung all the pans back in the cupboard and shut the door. Shoving Joe in his bouncer chair, she grabbed her cup of tea and began bouncing him, just as the door flew open and Tasha ran in full of excitement about all the presents they had found.

'I'll just pop him up for his nap, then you can show me what you've got,' she said smiling at them both and left the kitchen. Wandering back up the stairs, she couldn't believe what she had actually seen. Rocking him to sleep, she put him down in his cot and popped the baby monitor on.

'Gosh, you have really spoilt him - he's so lucky to have you as a big sister, that's for sure,' she said, as she was shown all their shopping. Handing them some scissors and Sellotape, Joan started making his birthday cake while Tasha and Amy wrapped all the presents.

Lying in bed that night, with Joe fast asleep beside her in his cot, she suddenly felt a small amount of hope. Maybe that room would be her way out, she just had to work out how.

Over the next few months people began to relax more around her, and Joe made life bearable being such a happy baby and lots of fun. He also helped take her mind off things, even if it was just for a short time, and allowed her to access areas unavailable before, as crawling and totting everywhere, she could claim 'Sorry, I only turned around for a minute and he was gone!' It gave her an opportunity to work out how things ran and to begin her escape plan, while everyone was so happy to see Joe and have a cuddle.

Having recently spent time at the garage and pub, she had also wandered up the road past the cottages. In daylight, they all still looked to be empty but she had to check, conveniently steering Joe up each footpath, he giggled as they knocked on each door, calling out and pretending to look for Tasha in their latest game of hide and seek. *How strange that no-one else lives here, not even that old man,* she thought to herself. Taking their seats on the trailer, as Kevin approached to get in the tractor and drive them all back to the farm for tea, she asked, 'Does no-one live in any of those cottages then?'

'No, why?'

'Well, maybe one day I could move into one of them, you know with Joe as he gets bigger. We could help you at the garage more often then too?'

He didn't answer.

At any opportunity, she snuck into the secret room to study which screen covered which area, but more importantly to try and work out what the switches were for. Each time she chose one, and clicked it on, a screen came to life panning around the area it covered. She had to be careful, so took notes and clicked it off again and left the room, before anyone could tell.

It was only when she pressed buttons four and five that everything fell into place. While button four showed various road signposts change direction, it was button five that truly shocked her. A gateway to a field, that looked completely overgrown, opened and with the scenery suddenly sliding out of the way, a road was exposed. The road down to the garage, the road she and Lisa had taken. But how did they direct them again on the way back?

Hearing a voice calling out, she quickly pressed both buttons again and rushed back into the kitchen. Stood there, ready to greet Tasha, Joe put his arms out for a cuddle with his big sister, which instantly covered any oddness. 'I'm hungry, can I have something to eat?' said Tasha.

'Of course, what do you fancy?' asked Amy smiling at her and they both walked over to the fridge to see what was available. And suggesting Tasha took Joe through to the lounge to play while she made her cheese on toast, she quickly double-checked everything in the secret room was back in its original place and pressed the switch to close it up again.

While Amy was figuring things out on the quiet, everyone seemed completely oblivious. She hadn't tried to escape for such a long time, so everyone just carried on with the daily routines of running the farm and garage.

With the setup being so complex, she knew she would only have one chance. She'd been thinking long and hard about how it could work, but also that she could only take Joe with her. Tasha would have to stay.

What she hadn't been expecting was Tasha to wander in with some news. 'I'm not supposed to tell, but me and Charlotte are going to have another sister,' she whispered and put her finger to her lips. 'You won't tell on me, will you?'

'No, of course not, but are you sure?' Amy whispered back.

'Nanny says she should be here next week, if she's not late. I'm so excited!'

'I expect you are. So where is Charlotte's mummy now?

'Well, I thought she'd left... like the other mummies. But she must have come back mustn't she? I haven't seen her yet though,' she replied, passing a toy to Joe to keep him happy.

'But isn't she your mummy too?' Amy asked quietly.

'Oh no, but we both have the same daddy.'

'What Kevin?' exclaimed Amy.

'Yes, why do you say it like that?'

'Oh, sorry, no reason, I just didn't realise that's all,' Amy replied smiling, thinking Charlotte looks nothing like Kevin or Tasha. But she looked a lot like Mark, up at the other farm, and she guessed that was the real reason she lived up there.

Ten days later, Joan and Tasha left to go to the shops - Charlotte's new sister Emma had arrived. They'd been popping up there more and more over the past week to see how things were going, and with Joe teething and screaming the place down, they were happy to leave Amy and Joe at home on their own.

Spending as much time as possible studying the screens, with Joe playing on the floor, she had realised they were completely cut-off from any other people. The two farms covered an extensive amount of land, with just the odd outbuilding dotted around, and the garage and pub equidistant between them. And watching all the screens, she also learned that whilst there were quite a few children (mainly boys) bouncing around the farms and fields, there didn't seem to be any young women. She'd heard Joan telling Tasha many times about how she would take over running the farm when she was older. And then she could have her own family here too... continue the family tradition. That's why they were so pleased that *at last* they were having some baby girls in the family. For ages it had just been boys being born, at which point Tasha said 'Girls are better aren't they Nanny?'

'Well, only girls can have babies...' she answered her smiling.

But there was one particular anomaly that Amy hadn't worked out yet. At both farms, there was a small red dot flashing in the top corner of the screen but there weren't any on the other screens. What could it mean? And she still hadn't been brave enough to try any of the switches, worried that they might set an alarm off or something, alerting everyone to the fact that she had found the room.

Two weeks later, Amy got to meet baby Emma. Carrying her into the lounge, Tasha sat on the floor with Joe, while Joan passed Emma over to Amy for her first cuddle.

'Oh she's adorable isn't she,' Amy said smiling at her dear little face.

'Perfect, isn't she - we couldn't be happier. Another girl too,' Joan said beaming. 'Not that we don't love Joe, of course we do, but to finally have another girl in the family means the world.'

Amy just looked down at the little baby in her arms, instantly feeling worried for this little girl's future.

'And how's her mum doing?' Amy said, looking directly at Joan.

'It wasn't an easy birth. She is resting and we are all hoping for the best.'

'Oh my god, is she in hospital?'

'No need, the doctor is taking care of her.'

A few days later, asking how Emma's mum was doing, she was told that she had taken a turn for the worse and sadly passed away. 'Please don't mention it to the girls though; we don't want to upset them. *No-one* is to say a word,' and with a stern look, Joan left the room.

Amy's mind was racing. Lying wide awake in the early hours with Joe quietly sleeping next to her, she thought she heard voices. Standing next to her door, she overheard Kevin talking to Joan on the stairs. 'I told Mark to find someone else, knew she was going to be a nightmare. Thank god we got lucky with Amy eh. Reckon it won't be long before we should try for another one, if we're lucky, a little sister for Tasha. Joe doesn't need her all the time now, does he - you can look after him for a bit!'

With her heart thudding in her chest, she tried to calm her breathing. 'Oh my god, I have to get out of here. Come on, come on, think!!!' she mouthed silently to herself.

The next morning at breakfast, Kevin announced, 'I've got a lot on at the garage for the next couple of days, lots of issues with machinery. Could do with some spare hands for running around fetching things, if anyone's up for it?'

Tasha moaned that she had to help last time, 'and Charlotte has invited me to stay over with her for the weekend, can I go... *please*?'

Looking at Joan for agreement, she and Kevin both said 'good idea' at the same time. Which instantly made Amy panic even more. Turning to her, Kevin smiled and said, 'Fancy giving me a hand? Joan could look after Joe if you like?'

'Oh he's had the runs in the night, bit clingy and poorly, so if you can cope with him being a bit smelly, I don't mind helping but he'll have to come too,' said Amy.

'Suit yourself. But Joan can come and get him if needed, can't you Joan?'

She smiled and nodded.

Hurrying upstairs, with the excuse of another nappy change, she was shaking. Stuffing essentials into Joe's changing bag, piling nappies and wipes on top, she headed back downstairs. She had to somehow get in the room.

Hearing Tasha scream that Nanny was hurting her hair whilst brushing it, and as everyone was busily getting ready for the day ahead, she quietly made up four of Joe's bottles. Popping them in her bag with a jar of food, she'd just finished as they arrived in the kitchen.

'Say goodbye to Amy, Tasha,' said Joan.

'Bye. See you on Monday... yuk, Joe stinks!' she said, pinching her nose.

'Sorry about that, yes he does doesn't he! Have a lovely weekend with Charlotte, Tasha.'

'I'll only be about half an hour, just popping her over there now. See you later,' Joan confirmed as they headed out to the car.

Dashing around the kitchen, grabbing a few snacks, she quickly changed Joe again just as Kevin appeared in the doorway.

'Ready?'

'Yep, I'll just finish sorting him out and I'll be there. Give me two minutes.'

'Sure,' and Kevin left to go and get in the tractor.

Entering the room and scanning the screens, everything was as it was everyday, except for the screen at Charlotte's farm - the red light in the top corner wasn't there anymore. There was only one here now. *'Haven't got time to worry about that now,'* she thought to herself as she pressed *all* the switches. Screens sprang into life, showing signposts changing direction, gates opening and roads appearing in odd fields. Hurrying back into the kitchen, she pressed the switch in the cupboard again and as the wall closed, prayed that no-one was any the wiser.

'Right you, home time today all being well,' she said to Joe, as she picked him and gave him a big cuddle. 'Please God, let me get out of here...' she whispered to herself, picking up her bag and heading out to the tractor.

'I've brought his pushchair for when he is tired, ok?' she said, heaving it up into the trailer.

'Fine,' replied Kevin.

They both sat in silence as the tractor trundled down the road to the garage.

As soon as they arrived, Kevin got to work on a jammed piece of machinery, leaving Amy to settle Joe in his pushchair. Her heart was racing as she worried that someone would notice that the switches had been activated, but for now at least, it seemed all was well. But she still had to think of an excuse to take Joe for a walk. *'Think Amy,'* she muttered, nerves in tatters. Whispering sorry to him, just as he was beginning to doze off she gave Joe a firm nudge, making him cry. 'I'm just going to take him for a walk up the road to try and settle him, ok?' she called out to Kevin as she stepped outside the garage shop door.

'Ok, but if he doesn't settle soon I'll give Joan a call - see if she can pop him back home,' was his reply.

With their bag on the rack underneath, she hastily began walking up the hill. Remembering the screen for this area, she knew once the button had been activated, a field gate opened and a road appeared to the left of the cottages. From there, she could run with the pushchair about half a mile to the top road. And then, if everything was still open, she needed to head in the opposite direction to the signpost, taking her all the way to the first proper B-road for miles. The cameras had picked up cars regularly travelling along this road, she'd seen them on the screen - she just had to hope that today was no different and Kevin was too preoccupied to notice her absence. Having tested the switches in turn, she also knew that once they were pressed again, it only took a couple of minutes before gates were covered over and everything returned to its original place.

But as they passed the last cottage and raced up the road, what she hadn't expected to see was a car coming towards her. Seeing Amy running in her direction, the young girl driving slammed on the brakes.

As Amy reached the car door, she pleaded with her to open it.

'Are you ok?' the girl said, alarmed at the desperation on Amy's face.

'No, *please* let me in and turn the car around. We have to go NOW!'

Flinging her door open, the girl rushed out of the car to help her. 'Please can you hold Joe?' asked Amy, passing him over while she quickly collapsed and threw the pushchair on the backseat. Getting back in the car, she said, 'My name's Amy, I'll tell you everything, but for now please listen to me. We need to get out of here.'

'Ok. What do I need to do?' the girl replied, sensing the panic.

'Turn around as quickly as you can.'

With the road being narrow, it took about seven manoeuvres before they were turned around and heading back up the road.

Arriving at the top road and the signpost Amy instantly recognised, she told her to go right and then the next left. Speeding along the narrow roads, Amy assured her that the chances are there would be little or no traffic. And holding Joe tightly on her lap, with her seatbelt around them both, they headed out of the area. 'Shouldn't be long now before we're on the B-roads and finally on our way home,' Amy said, looking at Joe with tears rolling down her cheeks.

'Thank you,' she said, looking at the girl.

But Kevin had just gone to look for her, and phoned Joan when he couldn't see her anywhere. 'Could she have just gone for a long walk?' asked Joan.

'You're probably right. I might be going mad but thought I heard a car. But we know that can't be,' replied Kevin.

'Alright, I'll just have a quick check on the cameras – see if I can see them. I'll phone you straight back,' and she hung up.

Entering the room to see all the screens on, Joan gasped. Seeing an old Fiesta hurtling towards the outskirts of their land, she slammed her hand down on one of the buttons, but it was too late.

'She's gone!' Joan screamed down the phone to Kevin. 'Get back here now while I let everyone else know!

'What the hell was that?' exclaimed Amy, at a loud clunking metallic noise.

'Christ knows!' said the girl, as they just cleared the metal rods that had been activated on the cattle-grid. Seconds later, they turned out onto the B-road and the girl's phone bleeped that signal was restored and she had a text message.

'Here, phone the police!' she said, handing Amy her phone.

'No, I can't trust them around here, they'll take me back. I need to get home to my mum and dad, can you help me?'

'Yes of course, now talk to me,' she said, clasping hold of Amy's hand. 'I'm Kathy, by the way.'

With Joe in her arms sound asleep, as Amy began talking she suddenly looked down to see her necklace from Tasha. Telling Kathy a little about her, and that she felt a bit bad that she had gone and left her behind, 'She even made me this,' she said showing her the necklace.

'Probably best to let it go Amy. Throw it out now,' said Kathy, holding out her hand to pass it to her. And chucking it out of the window, they were then shortly on the motorway back home, with Kathy insisting she would drive her all the way to make sure she and Joe got back safely.

'She's stopped!' Joan called out, standing at the screens. With the red dot flashing, she knew exactly where she was too. 'You get up there now while I finish off here. Get rid of her!' said Joan, and Kevin quickly left on his motorbike. Finding her necklace on the roadside, he sped along the roads hoping to catch sight of them but they were long gone. Slamming the necklace down on the kitchen table on his return, Joan picked it up, removed the GPS tracker and popped it in her pocket.

Stopping in a service station for a short break, they found a table tucked in the corner of the restaurant and while Kathy went to get them some drinks and food, she passed Amy her phone. A quick search and she was on Lisa's Facebook page.

Photos of them both on their weekend away with the two guys they had met on the Saturday night; breakfast on the morning of their departure and then a month's gap. Followed by so many comments, 'RIP Lisa, you'll be missed x,' 'Can't believe you aren't here anymore xx,' 'Gonna miss you, crazy lady... keep dancing until I see you again xx'

Another quick search and she was reading the local police report. She'd been found miles away, upside down in a deep waterlogged ditch in her car, with a branch impaled in her neck. 'Must have lost control,' was their conclusion. 'Passenger missing, still unaccounted for, but likely to be recovery of body rather than rescue after all this time. Searches have been withdrawn for now as after extensive coverage of the surrounding area, nothing has been found. We would like to thank the public for all their support and assistance, but do ask that you now leave us to support the families at this very difficult time.'

Scrolling back to the top in disbelief, she then returned to Lisa's page and her post about their pub visit on the way. 'Bloody satnav took us to the arse end of nowhere, ended up having lunch in a pub with inbred family that didn't even have Prosecco for god's sake. Bunch of weirdos, avoid at all costs, like something out of one of those horror films - remember Wrong Turn? The kid looks like she's probably a mix of all the family members! Lucky to get out ☺' and then an anonymous comment below... *'That's not very nice Lisa ☹*.

Kathy's arrival back at the table, with Joe desperate to grab everything on the tray, jolted her back to where she was. 'You ok?' she asked.

Shaking her head, she passed her her phone with both pages still open ready to read.

'Bloody hell,' muttered Kathy, taking a gulp of tea.

Half an hour later, having let Joe have a quick tot around on the grass before getting back in the car, they'd filled up with petrol and were heading down the slip road to rejoin the motorway again.

Back at the farms, everyone was frantically packing. 'Come on kids, we're going on holiday to Dan and Tom's farms again. Grab your toys, you've got twenty minutes to be at the car!' they were told, as all the adults rushed around.

Powering down the system, Joan pulled up the temporary wall and clicked in the fixings. Dragging the shelving into place, she then called for the others to help her fill the shelves. Two hours later, with the cars finally packed up, Dan, Tom and their families began arriving.

'Everything ok?' asked Dan.

'Yes, all sorted now thanks. I've left notes about the few changes we've made but other than that, everything is the same as it always is. Don't think we should be away too long - maybe a couple of months. Just depends how many visits you get.'

'No worries. No rush, we're always happy here. Tom has already gone down to open up the pub and garage. All our lot are super-excited about the piglets too, couldn't wait to come and stay and take over for a while.'

And swapping keys and lives, they left for their time away.

Staying near the beach was such a different experience for their children, 'All a good part of their education too,' Joan said smiling at Kevin, as they finally unpacked and set about preparing some food.

*You Can't Leave*

Wandering down through the fields to the beach, the children squealed with laughter. Splashing each other and running in and out of the sea, they were all so excited to be on their holidays again. While for the adults, they finally allowed themselves to take a deep breath.

'Jesus Christ, I didn't see that one coming did you?' said Dave, looking out at the sea.

'No, and we had such plans too. Such a shame. Still there'll be others,' Joan answered smiling at him. 'Just need to wait a bit, let things calm down.'

'And in the meantime, let's have a nice break away. Then we need to work on our security when we get back. How the hell did she find the room?' said Kevin.

'Don't know. But it's a lesson learnt for us, isn't it. You just can't trust them really. Promise things, especially after the bunker. But it just shows, you can only trust your family. To be honest, I really hoped she might be different, but there you go,' said Joan.

After watching the children wear themselves out, she called out that it was time to head back. 'We'll pop back down again tomorrow, come on now, time for tea!''

Knocking on the door, her mum nearly collapsed as she opened it to see her daughter stood there holding a baby. 'Oh my god, Amy... Arthur!! She's home!' and Amy heard her dad cry out and come running in from the back garden.

With Joe slightly squished between them, Amy's mum then took hold of Joe while Arthur hugged his daughter. And with tear-streaked faces all around, Kathy was then also welcomed into their home.

Sitting in the lounge, hardly believing that this was really happening, they thanked Kathy for bringing her home while

Amy tried to settle Joe. As he nodded off, Amy lay him down gently on the quilt her mum had just put on the floor, and slowly began talking. Shaking as she began reliving the trauma, her mum just held her hand. It had been nearly three years since she'd left and so much had happened. As she then went quiet, her mum quietly asked, 'So are you going to keep Joe, knowing that one of *them* is his dad?'

'It's not his fault though, is it? He's my baby and the only thing that has kept me going for months now, so yes I'm going to keep him.'

'As long as you're sure, we're here to help whenever you need us,' her mum answered. 'Say, why don't you move back in with us, love?'

'Thanks mum, I'd love that.'

But then the conversation moved onto the police, and how they must be told everything that has happened. They can then go and find them, arrest everyone and make sure it can't happen to anyone else. But that can wait until tomorrow, or the next day.

Insisting Kathy must have something to eat before leaving to go back home, her mum prepared them all a meal while Amy and her dad went upstairs to reorganise one of the bedrooms for her and Joe. Regularly stopping to hug her, they were both so emotional. And after seeing Kathy off, they all took a seat in the bathroom to give Joe a bath before popping him to bed.

Triple checking that yes, all the doors and windows were definitely locked, Amy was *so* on edge. With any odd noise sending her into a complete panic, Amy's dad slept on the floor in her room to try and help her get a little sleep. Then after a couple of nights, she calmed a little and asked if they could just keep their bedroom door open a bit instead, just for now.

Four days later, the police arrived at their home to talk to Amy. Her mum and dad took Joe out into the garden while she then began telling them what had happened. With the conversation being recorded and lots of notes taken, she was then asked if she could bring herself to go back with them, in their police car, to show them.

'They won't see you, but it will help us so much.'

Sensing her fear, one of the officers went and sat in the back of the car and shut the door, to prove you couldn't be seen.

'How about I come as well? I'll be with you the whole time,' suggested her dad.

'Ok then,' and the following week, they were picked up early for the drive down.

Recognising some of the signposts after leaving the motorway, they were soon heading down a road, past the cottages. 'Stop! Go and look through the windows. You'll see no-one lives in any of them, everything is covered in sheets.'

The police officers pulled up and walked to one of the front doors just as it opened, and two little boys came running out, knocking into them. 'Sorry!' they called out as they ran off down the road.

'Hello. It's the police, is there anyone in?' one of the police officers called out from just inside the front door.

A lady walked through from the kitchen, wiping her floury hands on her apron and smiling at them. 'Er hello, can I help you? It's not my boys getting up to no good, is it?'

'No madam. May I ask whether you live here and if so, for how long?'

'*'Course* I live here. Me and my family have lived in these cottages for donkey's years. Why?'

'Er, sorry to disturb you,' and they walked back to the car.

Getting in, Amy gasped, 'This just isn't possible!' as she saw a couple arm in arm, wandering out from one of the other cottages.

At the garage, the shop was stocked up and a customer was paying for their petrol and a drink. The pub had four tables of people eating and a couple of older men, sat at the bar. 'Ok officer?' one of them called out, as they wandered in. Chatting with a couple of them, the landlord then popped his head out from the back asking if he could get them anything. Thanking them, but no they were fine, they walked back out to the car.

'You sure it was here?'

'Yes. I don't know what's going on but let's go to the farm...Tasha will be there, she'll talk to you,' with her heart now racing even faster.

Pulling up at the farm entrance, she recognised nobody. 'What is happening?' she exclaimed, in disbelief. After chatting with the residents, all the officers could do was thank them for their time and leave.

'It must have been somewhere else,' they said, as they got back in the car. 'We'll get a helicopter up to take some images of other places that look similar, that's all we can do for now.'

'Did you check the cupboards in the kitchen?

'Yes, we checked the cupboards and there was nothing out of the ordinary. No switches, no screens or anything unusual. They showed us the walkie-talkies they use to communicate with the other farms, but that's it.'

'What about Joe? Can't you take DNA swabs or something, test all the guys that live around here if you have to,' pleaded Amy.

'But you say you don't recognise any of them,' replied the police officer.

'But I was also unconscious, so have no idea who it was,' she said, suddenly going quiet.

After driving around for another half an hour searching the whole area, they left to return home. 'I just can't understand it, it doesn't make any sense,' muttered Amy, shaking her head.

A month later, the police were on their way back, with permission from the courts to do DNA testing. Visiting all the residents, with some questioning whether this was lawful until they saw the court documents, swabs were taken.

A week later, the results were back. 'Sorry, no matches. Could it have been someone you met on your weekend away?'

'No.'

The helicopter search proved fruitless. Three months later, they confirmed that the file would be closed for now until any new evidence came to light.

For Amy and Joe, with little other option, they needed to close this chapter on their lives for good. Counselling helped Amy, and with Joe and her parents by her side, just over a year later she started feeling more settled. The panic attacks had nearly stopped and she had begun going out without being a nervous wreck, thinking less and less that they were looking for her. She never went out on her own though. As a family they also decided that a fresh start, far away, would be the perfect reset.

Nine months later, they were pulling up outside their new home on the coast of Scotland. Having spent a number of weekends staying in B&B's, they found where they believed would be the best place for a new life, with a thriving local town and a lovely small primary school for Joe to join when he was old enough.

Kathy remains close friends with Amy and her family to this day. She was very honoured to be asked to be godmother to Joe and visits them as often as she can.

Elsewhere, systems have been tweaked and strengthened. They'd thought about taking Joe back, but decided not to. 'If it had been any of the girls, of course we'd go and find them. But let's leave Joe and put it down to a lesson learnt,' said Kevin.

Having paused their operation to let the dust settle, it's now been over six months since the last police visit and the skies are quiet.

And everyone is back and ready.

Signposts in place, ready to invite them to take a quick break in their journey. Potential ones will get to meet Dave in the pub, while Kevin fits a tracker to their car. The screen range has been extended so they can guide them back more easily, with the gateways and signposts synchronised to move into place at the press of just one switch. Necklaces have been upgraded so whilst they still track, they'll also set off the alarms the minute they go out of range and trigger their system shutdown.

Barry, the local police officer, is still happy to search their registration plate and let them know more about the occupants of the car.

And now it's just a matter of monitoring and waiting.

Both farms are eagerly awaiting their new arrivals.

# Not Long Now

*Not Long Now*

The day Daniel was born was full of mixed emotions.

While the proud new parents, Diane and Malcolm, cuddled their new baby boy, the midwives looked on wondering how on earth they would cope. Having lost part of her leg due to a complication of Type 2 diabetes, Diane relied on a wheelchair to get around, while Malcolm's back was now *so* bad that he needed a walking stick. But he insisted, 'It was no problem. He would push the wheelchair while Diane held the baby.'

'We will be fine, so keep your noses out!' he abruptly told the social worker who had also just turned up. And for Daniel's first year they seemed to be proving everyone wrong - he was such a contented, sleepy boy. With Diane none the wiser, after the first two weeks of getting little sleep, Malcolm decided to add a little something to his last feed of the day. *It was important that they all had a good night's sleep and no-one need ever know.*

And whilst Diane was ecstatic, as she never imagined they would be able to have children, Malcolm had it all planned out. Yes it would be tough, particularly on him, but this way neither of them would end up going into a residential home later on - their child could take care of them.

The problems only really began when Daniel started primary school and went to a friend's house for tea.

'Cor I love your bedroom!' he said, sitting down on the Star Wars duvet.

'Here you go,' said Callum, handing him a controller.

'Can I watch you first and then I'll know what to do?' asked Daniel.

'Sure,' and very quickly he got the hang of it. The bedroom was filled with squeals of laughter as they both worked together to defeat the robots and collect all the coins. Tea was delicious, by which time he didn't really want to go home.

But the knock at the door told him it was time.

'Hope you've been a good boy,' enquired Diane, with Malcolm stood behind her.

'A delight. Come again any time,' replied Callum's mum, smiling at them both and wondering how they managed.

Daniel never let on how his life was so different. He was such a caring boy and really only wanted to help his parents. He could see they were starting to struggle with almost everything, so was only too happy to fetch and carry whatever they needed.

Social workers were long out of the picture; having been happy with his development, he had been moved out of the 'at risk' category and, with no further reports of concern, his file was eventually closed.

His speech and language skills had help convince them that all was well. The place might be a bit scruffy, but watching him pick up his pile of books and plop himself down on his mum's lap, was all they needed to see. It was so lucky that his mum loved reading. Every day she would spend lots of time with Daniel sat on her lap, reading the same books over and over again. It was a special time that he would always remember fondly and be grateful for – just a shame things had to change.

He knew she had started really struggling with the pain, as she would lash out and then say 'sorry' over and over, explaining that 'mummy didn't mean to. It was just that her naughty body was hurting her *so* much.' He would give her a kiss and go and get her glass. Once she had swigged 'mummy's special drink', things would be better - at least for a short time anyway. Sadly, it didn't seem to work as well for his dad. Luckily Daniel was fast and quickly learnt to see the warning signs, getting out of the way and leaving the flat.

'Everything ok Daniel?' asked Adam, one of their neighbours.

'Get your arse back here!' his dad screamed out of the door.

'Yes thank you. Just need to pop to the shop,' replied Daniel, desperately trying to look ok.

'If you ever need anywhere to go or any help, just knock on my door ok. No. 65 on the next floor up,' Adam said quietly, smiling at him.

'Thank you Mr Adam,' he replied, dashing off down the corridor to the stairs.

Running into the playground at the bottom of their high-rise flats, he was relieved it was empty. Sitting on the swings, and going as high as his little legs would allow, he looked up at the sky hoping that one day he could fly away and go somewhere else forever.

And his dad was getting more and more cross with him. It didn't seem to matter what he did. The baked beans weren't hot enough, the spaghetti too hot – he couldn't win with the only two meals he could prepare without any help. They mainly lived on beans and spaghetti on toast, his specialities, and microwave meals – not bad considering he was only six years old. 'Callum's mum always cooks our tea for us,' he blurted out once but soon regretted saying anything.

He loved the time he spent at Callum's, but in their final year of primary school learned that Callum would be going to the local grammar school if he passed the entrance exams. Daniel tried to talk to his parents about him going there too, but was sternly told 'he wasn't to become such a snob. If the local comprehensive was good enough for them, it would be good enough for him.' And that was that.

Hurrying through the subway near his estate, with first day nerves kicking in, he kept his head down trying not to make eye contact with anyone. Trying not to breathe in the thick smoke, he gasped letting out his breath as he reached the other side.

'Blimey, wait for me!' said a voice catching up with him.

'Ravi! What you doing here? Thought you got a place at the grammar school too.'

'Nope, rubbish at Maths!' Ravi replied smiling.

'Hope you are in some of my classes then,' said Daniel, suddenly feeling a bit better that at least he knew someone after all.

Sat together at morning break comparing their timetables, it turned out that nearly three quarters of their classes were together, and so a special friendship began.

Ravi didn't have it easy either. Whilst his parents were very loving; running the local corner shop meant that they were often very busy. And some of the local lads were causing them problems, particularly because they were Asian.

'Why don't you come back to mine?' Ravi asked him as they were leaving school.

'Won't your mum and dad mind?'

'Nope, they often say how lovely you are helping your mum and dad. Come on!' and they ran off at speed.

Arriving in the kitchen to a batch of the most amazing cookies, they scoffed them down, grabbed a drink and went to say hello to Ravi's parents in the shop, before settling down in front of his games console.

Just over an hour later, there was shouting and Daniel could hear who it was coming from.

'Tell him to get his butt down here now!'

Sangita rushed upstairs to get Daniel. 'Your dad is here and not very happy by the looks of it,' she whispered, helping him grab his stuff.

'Your mother has been worried sick, you selfish boy!' his dad shouted and after a clip across the back of the head, Daniel thanked Ravi's parents and quickly left.

He wasn't at school the next day. Or the day after.

Ravi knocked for him but was told 'he was feeling poorly and couldn't come out to see him.'

The next evening, with both parents comatose, Daniel crept out onto the gangway for a bit of fresh air. Taking a deep breath in, he stood and watched a group messing about in the playground below. Giggling whilst handing around the bottle of alcohol, they larked about without a care in the world. 'Lucky them,' he thought.

Once the bruising had gone down, Daniel returned to school and lots of questions from Ravi. He hated lying but it was necessary.

However as time went on, and with the excuse of needing to do homework together, he soon became a regular guest at Ravi's. One evening, just as Daniel was about to return home, Ravi's parents called them both into the office at the back of the shop. 'How would you both like to earn a bit of money?' they asked smiling.

''Course, but depends what we have to do?' replied Ravi.

'Well, the local residents have been complaining about how awful the 'meals on wheels' service is nowadays. So with your mum being the brilliant cook she is, we want to offer evening meals for £2 each, that are delivered to people's homes. And we were hoping you two would like to deliver them. What do you think?' asked Arvind smiling hopefully.

Looking at each other nodding, they both said 'Sure,' at the same time, and the following week the service started. It created a real buzz about the place, seeing Ravi and Daniel with their trolleys laden with foil containers, charging up and down the gangways delivering all the meals. It was also a great way of checking everyone was ok. Word and the delicious smells spread quickly, and before long they were both rushed off their feet. Daniel also got to take free meals home for him and his parents.

Sangita and Arvind were always worrying about Daniel on the quiet. Seeing the conditions he lived in and hearing the shouting made them shudder sometimes, especially when they then didn't see him for a few days. He seemed to be poorly more and more often. Now he worked for them, they had an excuse to pop up and check on him if he didn't turn up.

One afternoon Malcolm made his way down to the shop to make a request. Finding that their mobility issues were affecting them more and more, he was struggling to get down to the shop for his regular order – vodka, special brew and cigarettes. He was delighted that his request for Daniel to pick them up for him (even though he was underage) was agreed straight away.

'I will put them in Daniel's bag so no-one sees. And as we know, the police never come onto the estate so shouldn't be a problem. He must bring the money with him though, ok?' Sangita said.

'Of course,' replied Malcolm, relieved it was so easily sorted.

For the next couple of years, Diane and Malcolm barely left the flat and this suited Daniel perfectly. He was there as little as possible. Meals and shopping were delivered promptly, leaving his parents happy and then an hour later barely conscious. He did his homework and had meals at Ravi's, followed by gaming if there was time, only returning home for bed.

The community 'meals on wheels' service was thriving and Ravi and Daniel were surprised at how much they loved their jobs. If there was ever an extra meal left over, Daniel left it outside Adam's door. 'He must be a bit lonely as always seemed to be on his own,' he thought, 'so he might like a little surprise.'

He would quietly tap on the door and by the time Adam opened it, would wave and put a 'ssssh' finger to his lips. Daniel would find out one day how much that gesture meant.

Daniel never let on that he earned some money from delivering the meals. His old piggy bank had been regularly raided by his dad in the past, so he knew to keep it to himself. He asked Ravi's parents not to say anything to his parents if they asked if he was being paid. They gave him a hug and found somewhere safe in their flat, just for him, to keep whatever he wanted. Sangita then quickly left the room so he couldn't see her tears.

As Christmas approached, the block of flats seemed the happiest it had been in years. Delivering the residents their Christmas Eve meals, Daniel and Ravi were greeted with gifts or a bit of money from most of them - it was an amazing atmosphere. A couple of people had put stereos out in the gangways and had carols blasting out, with everyone joining in.

Then came the shouting. Everyone heard it and the music stopped.

'Daniel, where the hell have you put my drink?!!' came hollering out from his flat door.

Hastily delivering his last meal, Daniel rushed his trolley back to the shop and ran home. Being shoved hard through the door, he set about finding the vodka. Finding and showing his dad the empty bottle, he had not expected to be hit so hard. Falling backwards into the side cupboard, some of the money he had been gifted tonight fell on the floor.

'Been stealing from me boy!' and whilst he scrabbled around to pick up the coins, his dad kicked him hard in the stomach. 'Bloody tea leaf, from your own parents too! Well to say sorry you can go and get me another bottle with what you have got there! Don't look at me like that, shift!' he yelled.

Daniel ran out of the door, trying his hardest not to show he was upset. People were still out watching and waiting to see what was going on and shook their heads, as he ran down to the shop.

Ravi's parents hugged him and passed him a tissue, whilst putting the bottle in a bag. They told him they were going to report his parents to social services and that he could stay with them if he liked. 'Thank you but I had better not. I'll be ok.'

Two weeks later, social services arrived for an arranged visit. 'Such a shame they just don't turn up,' thought Daniel. He'd been kept off school to clean the place and get everything ready. His parents answered all their concerns, and having been warned before they arrived, Daniel said nothing.

'Sorry to have wasted your time. Lovely to have met you,' said Malcolm, showing her to the door. Ten minutes later, Daniel got the hiding of his life.

Limping down to the shop to get their shopping, he vowed to run away one day and never come back. 'Please don't say anything again, I don't blame you of course,' he said to Sangita, with tears trickling down his cheeks.

'Oh my love, come here,' said Sangita pulling him into her, hugging him tightly. 'We are so worried about you, you know. What can we do?'

'Just stay as you are - don't ever change. I really don't know what I'd do without you, probably wouldn't be here,' and he left to take back their shopping.

A month later concerns were further raised. Daniel was now to be homeschooled as his parents needed him to help them a bit more. Well that was the story given to his school and the local authority. They had also stopped buying their shopping at the corner shop. They had a contact that would home deliver – cheaper too, nearly half the price.

The school were concerned and asked to visit them to discuss this further. 'No point, our decision has been made,' and Malcolm hung up.

The local education team asked to visit but were denied. Malcolm had read up that they couldn't insist on coming in and no checks could be made without his permission. '*Perfect.*'

Daniel's only escape was the 'meals on wheels' service. Having told them he was occasionally given some money from the local residents, Malcolm agreed he could carry on doing it as long as he handed the money over. Of course, Daniel put most of his earnings in his special drawer at Ravi's, handing over only a small amount. 'Bloody tight arses around here!' Malcolm would say, taking it off him.

Daniel was becoming more anxious about his parents' levels of drinking. Because with the increase, came more violence. Even his mum wasn't apologetic anymore and would give him a whack with Malcolm's stick if it was close enough. Life was thoroughly miserable and when the bruises and swelling showed too much, he phoned the shop to say 'sorry, he couldn't come in today.' Everyone on the estate could see what was happening, but couldn't see what could be done about it.

Having spent most of the past two days in his room, he needed some air. The knock-off drinks that were being delivered now seemed to be even more potent. So, after waiting for it to go quiet and seeing his parents completely 'sparko' he sneaked outside onto the walkway. Standing looking up at the moon and stars, he let out a deep breath.

'Pssst, Pssst!' came from above and he looked up to see Adam waving. 'You ok? Haven't seen you around for a few days?' he called down quietly.

As Daniel looked up, Adam could see he wasn't ok and raced down the stairs to stand beside him. 'I know the kids call me *'weirdo' and 'paedo'*, but I promise I'm none of those things. Why don't you come up to my flat for some time out?'

And for Daniel, as life couldn't really get any worse at the moment, he thought why not.

Walking into Adam's flat he was completely taken aback, it was so lovely and modern. He couldn't believe that anywhere could look like that, not around there anyway.

'Blimey, your place is really nice!'

'Cheers, did it all myself,' replied Adam proudly.

'Wish I knew how to do stuff, our place is a complete dump! I try my best to keep it tidy, but everything is old and tatty now. Mum and dad don't care. As long as they have got their drinks and smokes, that's all that matters,' he said, suddenly feeling a bit upset. It had been an awful few days.

Patting the sofa to take a seat, Adam passed him a can of coke and a controller. 'Well, like I said to you before, you are welcome here anytime. I want to thank you for the meals too, you have no idea how much it meant for you to do that for me,' said Adam, and with the game loaded, they began shooting the enemies.

Popping home a couple of hours later, Daniel felt better. His parents were still 'out of it' and it turned out Adam was great fun and caring too. 'Who knew eh!' he muttered, tucking himself under the duvet.

Daniel was desperate to pass his exams; it was the only way he could see of escaping one day and finding a new life somewhere else. He needed to be able to get a job and earn money, so somehow he had to continue his education. Luckily Ravi's parents had also been wondering how they could help him. So they decided that Ravi and Daniel should do their deliveries together, with Ravi's revision books put in the trolley for them to help each other on the way round. Arvind happily offered to help them both if they were stuck, assuming of course that he knew how to do it. And Daniel's parents were none the wiser.

Daniel found a phone number for the education department and asked where he could sit his exams as was being homeschooled. They agreed to make sure he was added to the list at his previous school and would send him the exam dates shortly – brilliant!

A few months later and with the exams nearing, he was trying to spend more and more time at Ravi's. He couldn't get anything done at home as there seemed to be more and more people dossing down at their flat. They weren't the type of people to be helpful either, quite the opposite. Whilst their lounge was filled with smoking, drinking and inane laughter, it meant he could sneak out, which was always very welcome.

While Ravi started having extra maths lessons after school on Thursdays, Daniel headed straight to No.65. It turned out that Adam was brilliant at science and was delighted to help Daniel with his revision. Unfortunately, someone else had noticed too.

'Oi! Off to see paedo again are ya?!' shouted Shane, seeing Daniel heading for his flat. Pedalling quickly to catch up with him, he grabbed the meal Daniel had saved and tipped it over him.

'Idiot!' shouted Daniel, flicking off as much as he could from his coat. He wasn't expecting the thump that followed and having had his bit of fun, Shane cycled off laughing.

Getting in the door he kept apologising.

'Doesn't matter, it's not your fault!' said Adam, taking his coat into the kitchen to clean it off. 'You alright though?'

'Yeah, he's just an idiot, everyone hates him. The ones that hang out with him only do it 'cos they're scared of him,' and sitting down with a drink, they started a game to take their minds off it. Science could wait for another day.

But Shane started hanging around more. One evening he watched Daniel put a meal on the floor outside Adam's and head back down to the shop. As soon as he was out of sight, Shane rushed up, peeled back the lid and tipped the contents on the floor before running away. Adam opened his door to see the mess left behind; unbeknown to Shane he had been watching him on his CCTV camera. 'You little shit,' he muttered to himself.

On the other hand, it was an absolute pleasure helping Daniel with his science. Pulling down some books off his shelf, he loved being able to share his passion. Ever since he could remember, he had found science fascinating and would regularly be found with his head stuck in one of his books. Just a shame nothing ever came of it.

\* \* \*

Adam wasn't any of the things he heard people calling him – 'nutjob', 'weirdo,' 'he's probably a bloody paedo!' He definitely would never be that.

At twelve years old, Uncle Jimmy had arrived into his world. Uncle Jimmy had been working overseas but had returned to the delight of Adam's parents. Welcoming him into their home, he was introduced to his nephew Adam, but Adam didn't like Uncle Jimmy one bit. Each time Uncle Jimmy came around, he had wandering hands. Finding out he was to look after him again while his parents had another night out, he found an old smelly sleeping bag at the back of the cupboard. 'This should do it,' he said to himself quietly, zipping it up tightly under his chin. It absolutely stank but he decided it was worth putting up with the smell. But it didn't make any difference.

When his uncle and dad popped down to the pub, he decided he had to say something to his mum – she could stop it happening.

'Don't you ever bloody say a word to anyone! He loves you and is just showing you that, he said you'd probably say something!' she snapped at him, clipping him around the back of the head.

'But I don't like it mum, please make him stop!' he cried out.

But she wouldn't listen. Apparently Uncle Jimmy was 'completely loaded' so if they kept him happy, one day their lives could really change for the better. 'So you just keep schtum. Anyway he's getting older now and not that well. It will be like winning the lottery when he goes, says he's leaving everything to us!'

While his parents were busy working, they didn't take the time to notice how miserable Adam had become. Spending most of the time in his room, he had become completely withdrawn. But his science teacher had noticed.

'Can you hold on a minute Adam?' he asked him, as the bell went and everyone piled out of the classroom. 'Are you ok? Everything ok at home?' he asked him quietly, looking a bit concerned.

'Yes sir,' he said looking down at the floor.

'Talk to me.'

'I can't say sir but thanks for asking.'

Filling in a form, his science teacher handed it to the headteacher and shared his concerns. He knew something was up. The following day, the headteacher spoke with both of Adam's parents on the phone and was reassured that everything was completely fine. Put down to 'hormones and moodiness –

lovely family, both parents work, lives in nice neighbourhood' were the notes made on his file.

Shortly after they received a letter to say Adam was now going to be homeschooled.

A lady from social services only visited once, after Adam had run away from home. Sat chatting with her cup of tea and slice of cake, she admired all the books they had bought for him to study at home and the gorgeous house they lived in. She offered to have him assessed for mental health issues or whether he may be on one of the scales they measure, but his parents reassured her that he was fine and they were keeping closer tabs on him now.

Listening from outside the room, as they finished their discussion and assessment of his behaviour, Adam couldn't believe it. 'Stupid bitch. Scale?! My life is completely shit and you want to assess me for mental health or something!' he muttered under his breath and crept back up to his room. Lying on his bed, he decided that something had to change and only he could do it.

Hearing the news that Uncle Jimmy had suddenly 'gone away again' for another few months, was a massive relief. He had to get through his exams, so started revising like crazy. At least he could now focus on this and not the dread of the next visit. And despite everything, Adam ended up passing most of them with good grades – an amazing achievement for someone who had received such little help. He quickly found a part-time job that would fit in with college, and for a short while his life became a bit more normal.

'Adam, guess who's here?!' his mum called out from the lounge, hearing him come in the door.

'Adam - good to see you,' smiled Uncle Jimmy, sprawled out on his sofa.

Adam ran out and up to his room. His mum flew up the stairs and flinging the door open shouted, 'How dare you be so bloody rude!'

'I don't want to see him mum and you bloody know why!' he shouted back.

'Well, you know how you have always wanted to go abroad. Jimmy has booked tickets for us all to go to Portugal, can you believe it? Just shown me the photos of the villa he has booked, it's gorgeous,' she said excitedly, expecting him to be the same.

'No thanks. I'm staying here.'

'Don't be so bloody stupid, of course you're coming. Jimmy insists. He also said that he is going to give us £100,000 when we get back to help buy a bigger place for all of us to move in together,' and she hurried off back downstairs.

Walking through the park late that evening, he was starting to panic. *How could he get out of going?* There was just no way. And after Jimmy's visit to his room when he got back, he finally snapped.

The next morning he got up and went to the library. But logging onto the computer his search brought up results he hadn't been expecting. Cases in court - 'Jimmy Collier was sentenced to twelve months in prison for child abuse images found on his home computer.' Rushing home to tell his parents, they of course already knew. Grounding him for a week until they leave for Portugal, he locked himself in his bedroom and cried so hard he thought he would never stop.

Waking up to a silent house, he crept downstairs to see everyone had already left for the day. He paced up and down the hall, thinking and planning what he could do. Packing a bag, and taking just one photo from the lounge of his late grandparents, he got to the door to find it locked and all the keys missing. Trying the windows, they were all locked too. Quickly grabbing a towel and putting it around the hammer from his dad's toolbox, he smashed the back window and left. Sneaking out of the back, so the neighbours wouldn't see him, he ran straight to the park to gather his thoughts. Sitting on the bench, looking out across the lake, he decided he would go to London and find some work. He had enough money from his savings to keep him going for a month or so; just needed to find a cheap hostel to stay in. And suddenly with a feeling of optimism that he was now taking control over what happened to him, he left for the bus station.

Walking along the back roads, he had no idea that he had been spotted. Lost in the thoughts of his plans, he didn't pay any attention to a car slowing up just behind him. Grabbed and bundled into the backseat, 'Where you off to? Thought you were grounded,' sneered Jimmy and with the doors child locked, he was taken back home.

His parents were furious - for thinking of leaving and ruining their future; for smashing the window and for trying to stop them from going on holiday. 'Bloody selfish you are!'

The early morning flight was in two days time and Jimmy was coming to stay over the night before, so they could all get ready together. It didn't matter how much he screamed and cried; they wouldn't listen.

He found the number for social services. 'Sorry love, I can't help you. Jane Allen is your contact and she has already left for the day. I'll ask her to call you tomorrow morning if that's ok,' and making her promise that she would phone, he hung up feeling sure that she would listen and help him. At least she could step in, knowing Jimmy's background, and move Adam to somewhere safe.

But she didn't call.

While the excitement was growing downstairs, panic had properly set in now for Adam. Hearing Jimmy arrive, he decided to do something or it would be too late.

'Hello, is the patient breathing?' asked the ambulance dispatcher.

'No, please come quick! It's my mum, dad and uncle – none of them are breathing!' and the sirens arrived shortly after.

Giving him a tissue to wipe away his tears, everyone was so sorry. They reassured him that he would be ok and someone would be arriving shortly to talk about what would happen to him. Wheeling the deceased out on trolleys, twelve hours later the room was silent again. Adam insisted that he would go to a friends' house while the teams finished all their investigative work. Three weeks later and post mortems completed, he stood with a few neighbours and some of their work colleagues in the crematorium.

The coroner's report showed they all had significant levels of alcohol in their system. The fire service reported that the gas fire in the lounge hadn't been serviced for years, and with a partially blocked flue, carbon monoxide had escaped into the room. They would simply have gone to sleep and not woken up. A tragic accident that no-one could have foreseen. Luckily for Adam, the blocked flue had been put down to poor maintenance.

For the next few years Adam lived quite a nomadic lifestyle. Spending much of his time travelling around the Greek islands, he drifted from place to place. With the money inherited from the house sale and his parents' life assurance policy, he'd decided to take some time away to try and get over everything that had happened. The years had affected him so much; he didn't trust anyone. If he didn't let anyone get close, they couldn't hurt him. But he never regretted what he'd done; and Jimmy could never hurt anyone else now.

In his mid twenties he returned to the UK and spent time picking fruit and vegetables on farms in the summer. A world away from what he had hoped and imagined; he had always wanted to end up in the science sector but it wasn't to be. His family had ruined his chances of that future.

One day he jumped on a train and decided he would just get off at a random stop and see where it took him. He wanted to find somewhere to live and settle; but somewhere he could be anonymous.

Grabbing a Lucozade at the corner shop and being greeted so warmly, he thanked them and walked out looking up. Yes it was grim, but he also got a good feeling about it. Two months later, he moved into No.65. Incredibly it was one of the few that was available to buy; the council needing the funds for maintenance.

\* \* \*

Daniel arrived excited to show him his exam timetable. But as he looked at the number of exams, the nerves started kicking in. 'What if I fail them all?'

'You won't. Your maths and English is so good, much better than mine and I passed. You should breeze the science too but if you want to pop up for me to test you, just come anytime.'

Adam was a lifesaver. He was so patient and tested him over and over again, so he was as prepared as he ever could be. Ravi had also started joining them, with them all having a laugh gaming afterwards.

Popping down to the shop the next morning, Ravi's parents gave Adam a hug and thanked him for helping the boys so much.

'On us, honestly it's the least we can do,' said Arvind, handing him his paper, bread and milk.

'You are so kind, thank you. I really enjoy helping them – it's a pleasure. Always thought about being a teacher but things just didn't work out,' he said smiling at them both, and picking up his shopping left to go back home.

That evening, after doing their meal rounds with three extra for them to have at Adam's, they were both getting so nervous – only two days to the first exam.

'Just take a big deep breath when you sit down and remind yourself that you know it. You have worked so hard and deserve to do well,' said Adam, remembering those awful exam nerves.

Two days later, Adam's door flung open with two beaming faces desperate to tell him all about it. The first maths paper had gone brilliantly – even Ravi thought so.

'The way you explained it meant I just got it. You really should be a teacher you know, you're better than any of the ones I've had,' and they snapped open their cans of Coke and took a massive swig. 'My parents even spent a fortune on extra lessons, which didn't help,' Ravi said, putting his arm around Adam's shoulders.

It felt great - for all of them.

A week later, and with four exams out of the way, the nerves had calmed a bit. Meeting up with Ravi to go to the school hall together, Daniel didn't expect to bump into Shane.

'Waste of time exams ya know! You'll always live in this shithole, no matter what. When people see your address, it's the bottom of the pile for you!'

Walking faster, they tried to ignore him but Shane suddenly grabbed Ravi's bag. Pulling out his pencil case, he opened it up and tipped everything into the puddle. Cycling off laughing, Ravi quickly bent down to pick everything up.

'I really hate him you know. He's always nicking stuff from our shop and says bad stuff to my mum and dad. When my dad had a go back, some of his family visited. Better to keep out of their way with that lot,' he said tearfully.

Helping him dry off all the contents, Daniel gave him a quick reassuring hug, checked everything still worked and they hurried off to school. The start to the day hadn't helped and the first English exam paper was so hard – Ravi was sure he had failed this one.

'Easier said than done, I know, but try not to let him get to you,' said Adam, hearing about the start to their day. 'It won't always be like this.'

Late that evening Adam headed down to the subway to see who was around. With most of the street lighting out, it was easy to remain hidden. So he watched. Watched who Shane hung out with and what he got up to. Intimidating the odd person who had dared to venture through, laughing at their fear as they started to walk a lot faster, he shouted obscenities until they had disappeared from sight. The other lads were no better, and there were two girls that didn't seem to mind him grabbing them whenever he fancied.

The subway absolutely reeked of alcohol and smoke, with litter strewn all over the floor.

Adam started watching Shane more and more. He terrorised most of the residents, if they dared to get in his way. The council and police did nothing. Adam approached some of his mates when they were away from him, warning them to stop it. They quickly scurried away, heads down, apologising but saying they didn't have a choice. 'But you do,' he said as they walked off.

Shane had heard that he'd approached his mates. Tipping over another meal at his door, he knocked and waited for an answer.

'Piss off Shane. What is your bloody problem?' snapped Adam, looking down at another meal to clear up.

'Stay away from me and my mates, that's all I'm saying. Mind your own bloody business or you'll have my family to deal with!' and walked off back down the gangway.

But hurting Daniel on the way to his next exam so he arrived late, completely broke Adam.

At midnight the sirens woke everyone up. Seems someone had taking a disliking to Shane and a baseball bat had left him battered 'black and blue'. With the CCTV never working and people too scared to go out in the evening, no-one had seen or heard anything.

Ravi and Daniel sailed through their final three weeks of exams and after the last one, arrived at Adam's door. Ravi's mum had baked a big cake to say thank you and his dad had supplied some drinks. After they finished their meal deliveries, the rest of the evening was spent celebrating together at Adam's.

Now it was the school holidays and they had a bit more time, Adam spent a few hours each day showing Daniel how to do some basic DIY tasks (he had learnt them from a kind family in Crete whilst picking olives). Daniel picked everything up so quickly, happily chatting away about what he would do if he had his own place. Daniel also introduced Adam to some of the regular customers on their rounds, who had mentioned they had some repairs that could do with looking at. Before long Adam and Daniel were in huge demand and the talking point of the flats.

From fixing things and the odd bit of painting, to putting together flat-packed furniture and working out why the TV had gone wrong, each day they would get back to his flat in time for Daniel to start his meal deliveries, arms filled with thank you cards and edible gifts. Adam would never accept any payment, he was just happy to help and be a part of the community.

Third week of August and the nail-biting opening of the brown envelope with their exam results had arrived. Having collected them from the hall, Ravi and Daniel stood outside with Adam and Sangita waiting in anticipation. And seeing the look on their faces meant the world. They had passed them all and both had good enough grades to do the college courses they wanted. That evening, Arvind put a note on the shop door about closing early at the weekend.

On Saturday he welcomed Adam and Daniel into their flat, locking the shop up at 7pm. With music playing and the table laid out ready for a feast, they all celebrated and toasted the future.

But as Daniel arrived home, the celebrations were definitely over.

'Blimey, who knew you would turn out to be such a brainbox!' said his dad, looking at the results sheet.

'Good eh!' replied Daniel, looking for some sign that he was happy for him.

'Good but useless! I mean, who needs grades to claim the dole?' he laughed. 'Piece of piss, and the more care we look like we need the more money we get. So don't get any bright ideas about college or anything like that. We're not bloody losing the carer's allowance we get for you being here,' he said, ripping the sheet into shreds.

'How could you?!' screamed Daniel and ran to his room. His dad arrived a few minutes later to tell him how it was going to be. Ten minutes later, he returned to the lounge to finish his bottle and roll a smoke.

Ravi and Adam didn't see Daniel for the next two days. Concerned he was going to miss enrolment day, Adam knocked again. Having not had an answer to his previous knocks, he wasn't going away this time. Patiently knocking and waiting, after ten minutes he tried the door. It opened.

Entering quietly, he whispered 'Daniel, Daniel – you ok?' and waited. With no answer, he ventured further in. God, it was awful. The smog and smell hit him first; only then did he notice two people completely out of it on the sofa in the lounge. Sneaking past the kitchen, he knocked on the bedroom door. One was empty, so Daniel must be in the other one.

'Daniel - it's Adam,' he whispered and slowly opened it.

Daniel was fast asleep but he could see his face. Creeping over to the bed, he gently nudged him whispering his name. Daniel opened the eye he could still see out of and gave a little smile. Quickly putting some bits in a bag, Adam picked him up and carried him out of the flat and into his.

His face was so bruised and swollen; he quickly found a straw and got him a drink. Daniel then explained what had happened. 'I haven't even got my results now either, the bastard ripped it into shreds. School told me to keep it safe as you can't get another copy!' he cried, tears spilling down his cheeks.

'I'll sort that, don't you worry. The main thing is you are safe. You can stay here with me for as long as you like,' he said, leaving to get the spare room ready for his new guest.

'Maybe Shane was right - I will always end up stuck in this shit estate!' he said crying.

'No Daniel, that's not going to happen. You will go to college and do the course you want,' Adam said smiling at him, reassuringly. If there was anything in his power, he would make sure of it.

The following morning they were woken to loud banging on his front door. Malcolm was raging and could be heard before being seen, demanding Daniel 'get his arse home right now!' Opening the door, Adam told him to get out of his face and

Daniel would come home when he was ready. The punch that landed in his stomach, he hadn't been expecting. Bent over double and slightly winded, it hurt a lot more than it should. He managed to shut the door just as Daniel arrived at his side.

'Are you ok? You suddenly don't look very well,' asked a very concerned Daniel, worried by the change in his pallor.

'Yes, just got a bad pain. Help me over to the sofa and give me a minute, I'll be fine.'

\* \* \*

The pains had only really started over the past nine months. Stocking up on indigestion medicine, he thought it must have been his diet causing all these problems. But as they had started getting more severe, he paid the doctor a visit. 'Probably gallstones' was the prognosis, and he was referred for a scan. There was quite a waiting list but 'if he didn't hear anything in the next eight weeks, to let them know to chase it up.' He left with some anti-inflammatory medication to help in the meantime. It had been three months, so he'd better chase up that scan. No need to say anything to Daniel.

But after an urgent scan, the results came through – it was bad news.

\* \* \*

Walking up to the shop a few days later, Adam was shocked. Arvind was out the front sweeping up glass while Sangita was busy scrubbing the door.

'Let me help you,' he said, picking up one of the cloths.

Sangita was in tears. The police had been called but were unable to come out right now. Their CCTV camera had been smashed but had captured a small amount of footage. And there was Shane and his dad.

Hours later, the police arrived, viewed the footage and took the photos they had taken of the damage. Shane and his dad were questioned and released whilst further investigations took place. The council insisted there was little they could do – there were no other flats they could be moved to and you couldn't just turf them out and make them homeless.

'Why not?!' shouted Adam, standing next to the council representative.

'You just can't,' he replied, and making notes returned to his car.

Shane and his dad strolled around the estate like they owned the place. They knew nothing would happen - it never did. No-one went out past 6pm anymore, so Arvind decided that after delivering all the meals there was no point in being open. He put a large sign up in the window notifying all his customers (and neighbours) that after Sunday he would close at 6pm every day. The only customers that dare be around after that time were the ones he definitely didn't want in his shop.

Adam accompanied Ravi and Daniel to the college enrolment day - he was nearly as excited as they were. Chatting to the teachers and some of the students, they were pleased to finally be able to choose to study the subjects that interested them the most. That evening, they all sat around Sangita and Arvind's table again, tucking into their food while discussing and chatting about their decisions. Their futures were looking a lot brighter.

Getting home later that evening, Adam was in considerable pain and couldn't hide it from Daniel.

'Shall I call an ambulance?' he asked, putting his arm around Adam's shoulders.

'No, it will subside shortly; I just need to sit for a minute.'

Sitting next to him, passing him a glass of water, Daniel was really worried. 'Is it worth seeing a doctor then?'

'Yes, I'll make an appointment soon. Please don't worry. How about you put the Playstation on and have a go; it will be a good distraction for me,' suggested Adam, leaving to pop into the bathroom to take a tablet.

Ten minutes later it began kicking in, so he could relax again and watch Daniel destroy the enemies on the screen. But just as they were getting ready for bed, there was a loud bang on the door - and there stood Malcolm.

'I'm sorry about before, please come home Daniel. Your mum and I need you,' he said, trying his best to look a bit remorseful. But too many things had happened over the years for Daniel just to accept it and go back. Being sixteen, he finally had a bit more control over his life.

'No dad. I'll pop in and see you both tomorrow if you like but I'm staying here,' he answered.

For a change, his dad seemed to accept this and said they would look forward to seeing him tomorrow then. Adam thought it was a terrible idea to go and visit, but Daniel wanted to give him the benefit of the doubt; they were his parents after all.

But of course it was all a ploy. Their friends needed a new runner that the police weren't aware of; in return, for being a base for their activities, their supplies would then be provided free of charge. Daniel hadn't realised that they weren't just drinking alcohol now. Hearing how much more Daniel could be earning, rather than the stupid meal deliveries, they had agreed immediately. The only person who was clueless was dear Daniel.

While Adam attended his emergency doctor's appointment, Daniel made his way down the stairs to his home.

'Morning Daniel love, come and give your mum a hug,' said his mum, smiling at him from the lounge.

Wandering in, he didn't know they would have company.

'Meet Saul... Saul, this is Daniel.'

'Hi mate, you alright?' said Saul, getting up to shake his hand.

Daniel wasn't stupid; something was up. Saul was Shane's older brother.

'Why would you ever think I would do that?! I'm off to college soon, are you bloody mental?!' he shrieked, hearing their idea.

'£800 a week you could earn. You'll never earn that much from a stupid college course!' said his dad, trying hard not to get cross and shout.

'Yeah, and end up like you lot! No thanks!' but of course, he wasn't really going to be given the choice. Quickly taking his keys off him, they locked the door and asked him just to sit and think about it; not go running off to his 'weirdo' new friend.

Feeling a bit outnumbered, he played along. Sat chatting, all the while thinking of his exit strategy, he desperately tried to think of a way of getting out. But suddenly his arm was jabbed and then it went dark.

Getting back to the flat, Adam was concerned that Daniel hadn't returned yet. By midnight, he was pacing up and down wondering what to do. He had stood outside their flat but it was silent. Trying the door, it was locked – damn! He rushed back home to get his copy of their key. Concerned about Daniel's previous visit, he had discreetly taken his house key to get a copy made while Daniel was doing his meal deliveries. So whatever happened, he could help.

Unlocking the door in the pitch black, as most of the outside lights had stopped working long ago, he quietly tiptoed into the lounge. As usual, there were his parents but also a huge amount of wraps, needles, cash and drugs. He quickly made his way to Daniel's room but couldn't wake him. Seeing a small drop of blood on his arm where the needle had gone in, his heart raced so fast he felt sick. Picking him up and creeping past, no-one even stirred.

He placed him down on the bed in his flat, quietly shut the front door and headed back out.

An hour later he returned to his flat and got into bed.

6.00am all hell was breaking loose on the second floor. 'Police! Get down! Lie on the floor with your hands behind your back!' and the van full of armed police crashed their way into Shane and his family's flat. Having had an anonymous tip off about drugs and weapons, they found enough evidence to arrest and charge them. They would be staying at His Majesty's pleasure for many years to come. They of course protested their innocence, but the evidence was indisputable. Neither ever worked out how the stuff got there; they were always careful to hide things. Shane never dared to tell his dad that the night he was beaten up, he had lost his keys.

It was only late the following afternoon, that someone wandered past Diane and Malcolm's flat to see the front door ajar. Calling out and not getting any answer, they crept in to find them all in the lounge. 'No, no-one is breathing. All their lips are blue!' was shrieked down the phone to the ambulance team.

Saul, Diane and Malcolm were found with significant levels of alcohol and drugs in their system. But cause of death was listed as carbon monoxide poisoning, and by the state of the flat, the coroner ruled accidental death. Apparently no-one had been allowed in to maintain the boiler or gas fire in the lounge – the owners would never allow it as they used to accuse everyone of 'snooping'.

Daniel shed a few tears - partly because it was his mum and dad but also for show. Inside the relief was immense. It was like the sun had come out and shone on him, finally. He could now go to college and have a future; no more feeling scared. Adam was happy for him to stay with him in his flat and the council had taken back possession of his old home.

The two blocks of flats, sat side by side, were now so peaceful. Residents wandered around freely; stopping to chat or sit on the benches by the playground to watch the children having fun. Having ok'd it with the council, Adam had then visited a local flower shop in the town to place an order. A week later, they arrived with tubs and troughs of flowers to disperse throughout different floors and surrounding areas; instantly brightening up the place. Adam watched and smiled as everyone came out so happy to see the changes taking place.

Daniel and Ravi both started their college courses, aiming for careers in medicine or laboratory work. Sangita and Arvind's shop was buzzing again, with the residents often popping in just for a quick chat and to check their meal orders. Everyone kept their outside areas spotless; feeling real pride in where they now lived - a loving community.

But for one person the clock was ticking; he had one last appointment to make.

He never wanted it to turn out like this, but sometimes we don't get to choose.

Dashing home one afternoon, Daniel found the door locked and a note stuck to the bell. *'Daniel, please don't open the door. Phone 999 and wait, love Adam xx'*

Frantically rushing down to Ravi's, he grabbed the phone and dialled. The ambulance arrived within minutes, whilst Daniel already knew in the pit of his stomach that it was bad. Adam had told him that the doctor was concerned and was referring him to the hospital, but never said he'd had an appointment.

As the ambulance crew came out and phoned the police, they couldn't really say too much. Just that they were sorry.

Daniel sat on the floor outside the flat, feeling numb. Silently sobbing, he didn't know what he would do without Adam. He had meant everything to him. And now he had no-one.

The police officer arrived and went into the flat with the paramedic. Within fifteen minutes they came out to talk to him and confirm Adam had taken his own life. 'Overdose, he would have just fallen asleep.'

Adam had left three notes on the coffee table: one for the police, one for Daniel and one for Ravi and his parents.

*'Dear Daniel*

*This is by far the hardest letter I have ever had to write. You have been like a younger brother to me. You are such a lovely, caring, clever lad who will do so well (that I am sure of).*

*I am so sorry to have to leave you like this.*

*Three months ago the hospital told me that I had terminal cancer and just a short time to live. I had two options: go into a hospice or help make a difference to someone that I care about more than anyone else. Easy choice wasn't it. You will never know how much it meant, the day you started leaving me a meal. It meant the world. Until that time I was completely invisible or someone people called names, no-one ever took the time to get to know me. But you changed that.*

*I hope in your life you achieve everything you want and more. I will be willing you on, from wherever we go to from here. The flat is yours now, my solicitor will sort out all the paperwork and be in touch with you soon. I have also left you a bank account with enough funds for you not to worry while you are at college, actually if you don't go completely crazy it should last you a long while* ☺

*Thanks for everything Daniel, I will never forget you,*
*Love Adam xx'*

Daniel couldn't speak. He just sat staring at the letter. The paramedic took a seat next to him on the floor and put his arm around him. 'I am so sorry.'

Tears streaming down his face, the next door neighbour came out and let the paramedic go. Ten minutes later, Arvind had taken his place and getting Daniel to his feet, took him back to their flat. Daniel would end up staying with them for the next six months. Arvind then showed him their letter.

Adam had been left a large inheritance from an uncle that he could never spend. He wanted them to use it to setup a community kitchen and cafe to support all the local residents. 'It must be somewhere safe for them to meet up with people and grab a bite to eat if they wish, and where everyone is welcome.' The deeds for the boarded up unit next to their shop were included; Adam had bought the unit in the hope that this would be ok with them. A substantial bank balance was included for the work and to cover at least the first few years while it got established.

The whole community was in shock.

Adam's funeral was packed, with two coaches arranged so everyone from the flats could say their goodbyes together.

Thanks to Adam, the estate has thrived ever since; with the new tenants of both vacated flats absolutely loving living there.

'Adam's Place' is now a hub for everyone... no-one ever feels alone now.

# Another Time

*Another Time*

I'd dreamt of this day for so long...

Mum cupped my face in her hands, kissing me, and then hugging me so tight. I just melted - it had been such a long time. The moment was only interrupted by my dear dad. 'Must be my turn - come here you!' he said, embracing me.

And then, there was everyone else - such an amazing welcome for my return home.

Later on, a large get-together had been arranged, catching up with people I hadn't seen for such a long time. Lots of laughter and tears filled our time together.

I stayed with mum and dad for a while, before they showed me to my own place which was very close by.

It was a long while, before it was *my* turn to be at someone else's welcome home. The week before, we were all informed it was going to happen. Each receiving a special message as we returned to our homes that day, it gave us all time to get ready. Seeing her picture on the message made me feel quite emotional.

After breakfast the following day mum and dad came to take me to the welcome area, so I knew where it was, and then it was time to think about her arrival.

It was so exciting helping choose the perfect music and colours to greet her. With the area flooded in orange, yellow and white flowers and the music playing quietly in the background, it was like being in a dream.

Then it was time...

We were all gathered together in a semi-circle, and then there she was.

I gulped, letting the tears flow. Wanting to rush to her, but not wanting to be selfish, I left her mum, dad and sister to have their first embraces, waiting patiently for my turn.

And then it *was* my turn, her tears matching mine and the biggest smile.

'I can't tell you how much I've missed you – there aren't the words,' I said, hugging her so hard.

'It's *so* good to see you, it has been such a long time. To be honest, I never really thought this day would happen,' Kathy replied, her arms wrapped around me with tears trickling down her cheeks.

Then standing aside, I said, 'There is so much to catch up on but I must let everyone see you first. We have all the time in the world now.' And after everyone had had a little time with her, we all drifted off, leaving her to settle in with her mum and dad before visiting her again.

My best friend Zoe's arrival, on the other hand, couldn't have been more different.

Getting home to find a note put through the front door, I was in shock. I ran up the path to her mum and dad; they had just received their message too.

'I can't understand it, she wasn't due for ages yet,' said Zoe's mum, rushing to get some things together. 'This is new to all of us, so I don't know what I need to get ready.'

But Zoe had already arrived.

Only her mum and dad were allowed a short time with her, there would be no proper 'welcome home' just yet. It seemed ages before I was allowed to go and see her. Apparently she needed to come to terms with what had happened and be helped with that, before rejoining all of us and starting afresh.

I was initially sad, then worried, then a bit cross with her. But that had to wait until we could spend some time together. I had so many questions.

'I just couldn't cope any more, being left on my own. It all got too much, I had to escape. I did leave a note though,' she explained, feeling very sorry. It ended up being quite a long time before she joined us all, to give her time to process everything that had gone wrong.

But eventually it *was* time for Zoe's get-together and at last, her proper 'welcome home.'

And it wasn't long after that that we all had our own homes, our work and a most welcome feeling of being completely settled again.

I have to say I absolutely loved my new life, particularly being with the children. Not being able to have children of my own in the past, I was offered the chance of spending as much time as I liked looking after them at The Centre - apparently people like me were always given priority. And some of them even decided to come and stay at my home for a while, which was *so* exciting.

Having asked them a few questions on the quiet about what their favourite things were from their other home, mum and dad helped me get my place ready. I wanted to make sure we had lots of fun, as well as lots of reassuring cuddles when they remembered things from their past.

But I also knew it was only ever temporary.

The first time I stood at their welcome area, holding their hand, waiting for their parent's arrival, was one of the most emotional times of my life. As they rushed to embrace each other, my eyes filled with tears, such happy tears... seeing both their faces. And then the thanks I got for taking care of them until they could be together again; there are no words to express how this feels.

So life continued.

A very happy life.

I had no idea that that was about to change.

Being invited to my review with my mentors, the comments were glowing and the checklist in front of them had virtually all the boxes ticked.

But it wasn't the same for Zoe.

Unbeknown to me, she had already had her review and her sudden departure and arrival here, had meant she hadn't completed her goals this time, so she *had* to go back.

Distraught at this prospect and insisting she couldn't do it, they had a proposal.

They just needed me to agree to it.

'We can't make you go, as it isn't really for your benefit, but it would mean the world to Zoe. She really feels she can achieve what she needs to, with you by her side.'

'But to leave everything here again... and it was so hard before,' I sobbed.

It was the hardest decision I had ever had to make.

'Don't decide right now – there's no rush. Just think about it, and if you need to chat or discuss it with us, our door is always open.'

Sitting with those closest to me, everyone agreed it had to be my decision. But they also could see how much it could further Zoe's life and it would definitely be the last time (for me anyway).

So after much angst and thought, I asked for another meeting with them and Zoe.

'Oh Hannah! I don't know how to thank you!' exclaimed Zoe, hearing my decision.

'But you have to promise me to stick to it this time – no matter how hard it gets. I'm not going to do this again,' I replied.

'Promise! With you with me, I know I can do it!' and she excitedly flew out of the door to tell her family the good news.

Our farewell was packed, so many turned out to wish us well.

And then before I knew it, the two of us were standing ready to return, waving our goodbyes.

'You go first,' said Zoe.

'No, you go first – just in case you think about changing your mind.'

Taking hold of my hand and looking at me, Zoe's last words were, 'Well they look nice don't they?'

'Congratulations Elaine and David, you have two beautiful, healthy girls.'

Matilda (Zoe) was born at 5.36am, shortly followed by Alice (Hannah) at 5.42am.

Having gone through four rounds of IVF, they were both in tears.

'Look at them,' whispered Elaine, staring at them both in the little bed on the trolley. 'The day we thought would never come.'

And while they were both very different, non-identical twins, they definitely had a strong bond.

Life took many twists and turns for both of them. And whilst they often disagreed, the falling out was never irreparable. Arguing over whose turn it was, through to choice of boyfriends and not helping mum and dad enough, they always somehow made it work in the end, and ultimately were always there for each other.

Losing dad though, shortly followed by mum, was truly devastating.

But Matilda held it together when Alice was struggling.

Alice's husband walking out when their daughter Ellie was only four years old, having only buried mum and dad the previous year, hit her so hard. Her rock had left. But she still had Ellie, and Matilda of course.

With Matilda now living on her own, after her last relationship had ended badly, she insisted that they move in with her. But a few pains that Alice had ignored during all the upset, turning out to be breast cancer, was the news no-one was expecting.

Putting a brave face on it (well at least when Ellie was around), promising 'mummy would be ok and not to worry,' Matilda took care of them both. And she was amazing. Like a second mum, or the best auntie in the world, she took over the school runs and everything involved in the life of a seven year old, so Alice could concentrate on getting better.

Which she did. But after three years, the scan showed the cancer had returned and spread, with palliative care the only option now.

Her dream had always been to be near the sea, so Matilda, Alice and Ellie packed up their lives and found a tiny cottage by the coast.

Wheeling Alice down to the beach, they all sat on a bench quietly watching the waves crash into the rocks.

'Can't believe it's your eleventh birthday next week, Ellie! Any ideas of what you'd like?'

But Ellie just wanted her mum to get better.

Wandering into the kitchen on her birthday, Alice was sat at the table with Ellie's presents piled high for her to unwrap.

Making them both a drink, she gave Ellie a massive cuddle before they both took a seat.

'Where's Matilda?' asked Ellie. 'Shouldn't I wait for her to get back before opening them?'

'She had to pop out, she won't be long. She said it's up to you if you want to wait or open them straight away.' So Ellie decided to wait.

Half an hour later, there was a knock at the door. Ellie dashed up to open it, and there was Matilda, stood holding a cardboard box.

'This is just for you,' she said. 'Careful with it,' as she passed it over to Ellie to take to the table. Something was moving around, and then with a little bark, a head popped up through the top.

'Oh mum – look!' she squealed, as she lifted out a black Labrador puppy. As it frantically licked Ellie's face, Alice quickly grabbed her phone and took a photo.

'She's gorgeous, isn't she!' said Alice, as Ellie handed their new addition to the family over to her for a cuddle. 'So what are you going to call her?'

'Um... Lucy.'

Daily visits to the beach were now spent watching Ellie charging in and out of the waves with Lucy. As Ellie waved to them from the water's edge, Alice took a deep breath. 'I don't think I have long now,' she said to Matilda, with tears filling her eyes.

Tucking her blanket over her, Matilda put her arm around Alice's shoulders giving her a strong hug. 'No-one knows though, do they?' she replied quietly, kissing the top of her head.

'I've just got a feeling that's all... and the pain is definitely getting worse.'

As they watched Ellie putting Lucy's lead back on, to make her way back up to them from the beach, they both wiped their eyes and were all smiles ready to greet her.

A month later, having had an amazing day together filled with fish, chips and ice-creams at the beach, Matilda and Ellie left Alice to have a rest. Reassuring them both that she was fine, just a bit tired, they went downstairs to get dinner ready. But when they returned to her room, Alice had passed away. Lying there looking so beautiful and peaceful, like she had just gone to sleep, any sign of pain was gone now.

The months that followed were desperately hard for Ellie and Matilda. After the funeral, they both tried their best to keep each other going. Mapping out a new life without Alice was so sad, but they didn't have a choice - like she hadn't got to choose either. But fulfilling her last promise to Alice, Matilda felt blessed to have been asked to become 'mum' to Ellie, taking care of her and Lucy too.

Celebrating her 40th birthday without Alice (the first birthday without her dear twin sister), it hit so hard that she was really gone. Both she and Ellie tried their best to have a happy day, but both ended up in tears.

But as has to happen, life has to go on, and they had to learn to live without her. And as hard as it was, they also learnt to laugh again and have good times. From watching Ellie in her school plays and clapping madly at her awards ceremonies to nervously meeting her first boyfriend – oh how she worried, and all the while hoping Alice would be proud of them both.

*Another Time*

'You look absolutely stunning Ellie,' said Matilda smiling, whilst trying desperately to stop mascara from running down her face.

'Ready?'

'If you are...'

And years later, she would sit quietly in her lounge, with just the clock on the mantelpiece ticking, fondly remembering walking Ellie down the aisle – one of the most beautiful moments of her life. And she would desperately try to keep focussing on those memories, and not the chemotherapy and cancer three years later that would take Ellie's life, just like her dear mum.

Matilda never left the cottage.

At the grand old age of ninety-seven, she went upstairs to bed for the last time. Falling asleep with a smile on her face, she was found a day later by a kind neighbour checking in on her.

The local hospice put a bench in their garden in her memory, thanking her for all her kindness and support. Always helping out at their local fundraising events, and baking her legendary coffee cakes for as long as she could, she also held the hand of so many in their final hours.

And for Matilda, the queue of people waiting to greet her back home this time said everything.

# You Should Have Listened

'Matthew Watson, this court hereby sentences you to three years in prison. On release, you will be put on the Sex Offenders register and required to attend regular appointments with the probation service. The police will also have to be notified of any relationships you enter into, for the safety of the public.'

Handcuffed, and shaking from head to toe, Matthew was led away to the van waiting underneath the court. 'But I haven't done anything, why won't anyone listen?!' he called out, looking at the judge and security guard.

'Yeah, you all say that,' was the only reply and he was driven away.

And so began his worst nightmare. His fellow inmates repulsed him; so not wanting anything to do with them, he kept his head down, sat on his own and most of the time refused to leave his cell. Barely touching his meals, the doctor had been called as his weight loss was so extreme. 'Physically he's fine - it's just his mental state and lack of nutrition. I've tried to have a chat with him, but got little response. He just keeps muttering that 'he shouldn't be here'. So for now, just give him these sachets as a drink.' But for Matthew, he couldn't care less. The worst part was his brother's refusal to come and see him. He hadn't answered any of his phone calls and he never received a reply to his letters. For the first time in his life no-one had his back. *Why wouldn't he listen and believe me? He should know better than anyone that I would never be interested in that sick, abusive world.*

A week later, the emergency alarms were pressed and cells quickly locked as the prison officers ran down the gangway.

'Matthew, can you hear me?' said one of the prison officers, undoing the sheet from his neck.

Tears trickled down his cheeks as he regained consciousness and realised he had failed. A week later he still hadn't spoken, but with his cell now very barren he just sat looking around, resigned to the fact that he was probably going to have to stay here after all.

Then three months into his sentence, he had an unexpected visitor.

'Things ain't going to change mate... you're going to have to start getting a grip you know,' said Jim, one of the prison officers, who had just taken a seat next to him on his bed.

Jim had been one of the few to really start listening as he began to offload. The events still shook Matthew to this day - the police pounding on his door, seizing his laptop and arresting him, while he had no idea of why they were there in the first place. They even had various fuzzy CCTV images showing him entering the flat at times that matched the images. He couldn't explain how the images were there, and 'Yes I do live on my own and it is my computer, but that doesn't bloody change anything... they are nothing to do with me!' Matthew had screamed at them, but they still wouldn't listen.

Jim didn't know why, but his words had really affected him. So many always protested their innocence, which no-one took any notice of, but something about Matthew was different. He caused no-one any bother and was a model prisoner too. Jim was also worried that with another thirty-three months to go, he wasn't sure Matthew would cope. His brother having nothing to do with him seemed to have left him completely broken.

'What do you normally do in the outside world – for a job I mean?' he asked Matthew.

'Customer services, why?'

'Just thinking. We need to help you fill your time here and also find you a distraction. Ever thought about training in anything else?'

'No.'

'Well you've got lots of time to think now. I'm off for the next couple of days, but when I'm next in let me know what you've come up with. Reckon I might be able find a course for you to do... it could help.'

'Thank you,' and for the first time since he arrived, Matthew smiled.

Ripping up Matthew's latest letter without reading it, and deleting yet another message from his voicemail, James got ready to go out for the evening.

When he'd heard about his brother's arrest, he decided he was never going to visit him and promptly cut him off. It could ruin everything.

'Well, made a decision yet?' asked Jim, unlocking Matthew's cell door for his daily thirty minute exercise.

'Nope... but apparently I should hear about my appeal this week, so all being well I'll be leaving anyway,' he answered.

Of course, by the end of the following week having lost his appeal, he'd hit rock bottom and was, for a short time, put back on suicide watch.

A week later and as Jim was unlocking his cell door, he asked 'Is the offer still there? I think I've decided.'

''Course. So what you thinking then?' answered Jim, reassured by the slight air of optimism he had about him.

'Well, it's pretty obvious no employer is going to fall over backwards to employ someone with my record now - I'm not stupid. So maybe I'll set up my own business... you know, to at least start earning some money. People in my block of flats are always moaning about how long it takes to get a plumber to sort out their heating, so maybe I'll have a bash and see how hard it is to learn.'

'Sounds like a plan. Leave it with me and I'll see what I can do.'

With no other distractions, and eager to fill his time not thinking about where he was and the people he was in with, he studied day and night. Meals were now eaten, as he felt a bit more positive that he could actually start making plans whilst counting down the days and months. Busying his mind with all the learning, as well as thinking about a company name and where he could get a cheap van and tools, it helped him so much... planning for when he got out. Fortunately, unlike his brother, he had always lived quite frugally and so had a reasonable amount in savings.

*   *   *

For identical twins, in lots of respects they were like chalk and cheese. Whilst they were hard to tell apart physically, their personalities and worlds were so different. Whilst Matthew (being the youngest by two minutes) was happiest just quietly making his way through life, spending much of his time helping his neighbours and just pottering around outside of work, his brother James was rarely at his apartment. An incredibly successful stock broker, living the high life in the city, his world was filled with expensive dinners, wine bars and women. The odd visit to James's latest apartment always made Matthew smile, seeing the cooker still wrapped in cellophane. 'Why cook when there are all these amazing restaurants on my doorstep?! People to see, deals to be done!' James would always reply, grinning. He was so charismatic, everyone loved James. Matthew was very content staying in the background.

Growing up under the care of their elderly grandma, having lost their parents to murder-suicide at the age of seven, they survived by being together. Whilst she had agreed to raise them, she was very resentful of them being there and set about laying down very strict rules - it was a house of 'being seen but not heard.' But they managed to instil fun in their little world by having each other and a great imagination. With no cuddles, love or toys to play with, the only time they really looked forward to was the two weeks every summer, when she would take them to her log cabin by the lake and let them run free.

When they were nineteen years old, she passed away, leaving them everything. Whilst they sold her home and all the contents, they both agreed to keep the cabin. The best memories of their childhood were there and there was no reason to stop going.

As the responsibilities of adulthood took over, they gradually went their separate ways but always vowed to be there for each other, as together they could get through anything.

\* \* \*

At the end of his sentence, he was still so shocked and saddened that James had never contacted him... not even once. He could never have done that to James and he would definitely have believed him.

With a bit of money put in his hand to get home and his bag of belongings, he waved goodbye to Jim, thanking him and saying he would repay him one day if he could.

'Just do well!' Jim called out, giving him a quick wave back.

But getting back to his flat was when the real problems began. Walking up to his door to find 'paedo' spray-painted across it, he fought to gulp back the tears. Quietly letting himself in, he dumped his stuff and taking a deep breath, sat on his sofa.

Sitting in the exact same spot he had left over three years ago, he burst into tears, sobbing with his head in his hands. '*What have I done to deserve this?*'

Wandering down to the shop to get some groceries, no-one would look at him. A couple of lads on bikes shouted obscenities, but he didn't care about them. It was his neighbours... his friends. 'You know me better than that, you must know that they got it wrong! I'm going to prove it too, somehow!' he said to Betty, as she hurriedly crossed to the other path to avoid him.

'It was your laptop Matthew, it had to be you - hardly anyone else visits you,' she replied, hastily walking off back to her flat.

Everywhere he went, the response was the same.

Sitting in the local pub, trying to enjoy his first beer, you would have thought he had the plague. Voices quietened, eyes looked away. So seeing he wasn't welcome anymore, he quickly swigged it down and left. A week later, he put his flat on the market.

Fortunately it sold within a week to a cash buyer, and deciding to go into rented, the sale completed in record time. His probation officer had only allowed the move because of the circumstances and after vetting his new address. It was now outside of his catchment area, so he confirmed that at some stage a new probation officer would take over from him.

Locking the door for the final time, he felt so incredibly sad. No-one said goodbye and he felt completely on his own again.

He wasn't going to give up on James though. He must make him listen and get him to help prove his innocence, *he must know people.*

A knock on his door a year later, he opened it expecting his probation officer, but there stood James.

'Oh my god, look at you... you look so different with all the facial hair! Well, going to show me around then?!' James asked, hugging him tightly.

Hugging him back so hard, Matthew asked quietly, 'Why didn't you come and see me or answer any of my calls or letters?'

'You know I couldn't... think about it. You know my world, I had to distance myself or risk losing everything.'

'But the promise we made to each other - didn't that mean anything?'

'Of course it did, you idiot!' and he whipped out a bottle of expensive champagne from the bottle bag in his hand. 'Come on, time to move on now. And I'm going to be a part of that, it's the least I can do!'

Downing the champagne and opening another bottle of wine, they both began relaxing and enjoying their evening together, like old times. Listening to James's crazy business life and all the scandals over the past few years, it was time well spent not thinking about Matthew's time inside.

'Did you ever try and find someone to help me?'

'Yes of course, but it seems the evidence the police had couldn't be explained away. Did you ever offer another explanation as to how it was on your laptop? I mean, did you give it in for a repair or anything?'

'No, and I still can't work out how it could have happened. But I can promise you, I've been stitched up and I don't know why. I mean, as far as I'm aware, I hadn't done anything to piss anyone off,' and then chatting about how this fresh start in a new place had probably been the best decision, they agreed the important thing now was looking forward.

With his probation officer now visiting less often, he was able to spend more time focussed on the business, which was now really beginning to pick up. Having attended night classes to gain more practical skills after his release, he had successfully passed all his qualifications with distinctions. Popping into the local print shop, he'd put together some business cards and within two weeks the phone had started ringing.

The next few months flew past, with just the occasional meet up with James. Their worlds were so very different, and Matthew was happy not to spend a minute in James's. The appeal of the dinners, networking and 'mixing in only the top circles' would make him run for the hills. 'Not for me, thank you very much,' he said to himself smiling, as he sat very happily with his fish and chips from the local chippy in front of the TV, reading James' text about who he was about to have dinner with.

Matthew had managed to secure a few contracts with local businesses, looking after all their heating and plumbing issues, as well as taking over some of their building checks. He really enjoyed it and it also meant he got to know some of the office staff, realising very quickly how much he missed the human contact and office banter.

Answering the phone one afternoon, expecting it to be one of his customers, he was surprised to hear a new voice.

'Good afternoon, is that Matthew Watson?'

'Um, yes... who is this?'

'Hi Matthew, it is ok if I call you Matthew isn't it? My name is Monica and I'm your new probation officer. I've just been handed your file, so wanted to quickly introduce myself and arrange a visit to meet you in person.'

'Oh ok. When were you thinking of?'

'Well I'm happy to fit in with you, as I understand you are working. How about late one afternoon next week – looking at my diary, I can do any day to suit you?'

'Friday would be good for me, shall we say 4pm?'

'Great. I've got your address, so look forward to meeting you. See you then Matthew.'

'Yep, see you Friday then,' and he hung up.

He didn't know why he felt a bit nervous, but he did. Picking up some fresh cream cakes on the way home, he was sat on his sofa with slightly sweaty palms, ready for his visit. At just before 4pm, he opened the door to a pretty, smiling face that was puffing and panting. 'God, I'm so unfit!' she gasped. 'Sorry, this is so embarrassing but the lift looked a bit dodgy, so I thought I'd take the stairs. Maybe I'll risk the lift next time!' she said, still trying to catch her breath.

Taking a seat in his lounge, he got her a glass of water and waited while she got her file and pen out of her large bag.

'So how is life going for you at the moment?' she asked.

'Pretty good thanks. Got a few business contracts looking after their buildings' heating systems and carrying out health safety checks, so can't complain.'

'Good, good. And how are you finding living here?'

'Again, good thanks. Haven't really got to know many people yet, mainly keep myself to myself. You know, just usual stuff... work, shopping to get supplies, the odd takeaway. Apart from that, I watch a lot of TV,' he replied, with a slight smile. He was never sure about probation officers. Most were like the police and weren't very good at listening.

'May I ask if you are in or have had any relationships that we need to be aware of?'

'Yes you may ask and the answer is no. I haven't been in a relationship for donkey's years actually. Don't think that helped my case either, everyone thought I was a bit strange.'

She just looked at him. 'And do you think you're a bit strange?'

'No. Just because I'm not like my twin brother doesn't mean I'm weird. People always assume we must be so similar. Whilst we look identical, we are so very different. He's the one that has always had girls hanging off him, that's just not for me. I find it very hard to trust people not to let me down. Growing up, this was reinforced so many times - it became the norm. So I would say I put up a barrier, something to protect me from getting hurt. God, why I am saying all this?' he said suddenly, aware of how he was spilling out feelings he hadn't expressed with anyone before.

'Well, from the short time I have met you I don't think you're strange either. I read all your notes and you are very different to what I was expecting,' she said smiling and then taking another swig of her water.

Excusing himself, he arrived back with the cakes and passed her a side plate and a little fork. 'Gosh, thank you. I shouldn't but it would be rude as you have gone to the effort,' and they both sat quietly, tucking into their cake.

'Sorry I haven't got anything posher!' he said, passing her a piece of kitchen roll.

'Oh, I don't do posh!' she said grinning, delicately wiping the cream from the corners of her mouth and fingers.

After chatting a bit more, and having not had any company for such a long time, he suddenly said, 'I was going to pop out shortly and get some fish and chips for tea, maybe a bottle of wine. Would you like some?'

'Um, er, it would be a bit difficult. I'm not really allowed to have contact on a personal level with any of my cases,' she answered, blushing slightly.

'Oh, of course. I'm not sure why I said that – sorry to have embarrassed you or made you feel awkward,' he replied, now looking quite red and like he wanted the ground to swallow him up.

'Anyway, I'd better be off now. Thanks for your time Matthew and for the lovely hospitality too. I'll be in touch,' and putting her file and pen away, she headed for the door.

'I am sorry,' he said, opening the door for her.

'Don't be. I'm very flattered,' she said, with the loveliest smile.

Having read his entire file over and over, and now having met him, she couldn't believe this was the same 'Matthew Watson' that had been sentenced. With most of the images and videos being in category A (the worst), her brain was struggling to imagine how the person that had just offered her fish and chips, had got off on this.

And her curiosity never waned. While the rest of her clients, who most definitely had been guilty of their crimes, took up most of her time, she often found herself thinking about Matthew.

Arranging another meeting with him, with the excuse of him being one of her new cases, she needed to find out more.

'Sorry it's ended up being a late one,' she said, as he opened the door to her at 6pm.

'No problem... I'm not going anywhere anyway.'

'Tea, coffee or wine?' he asked.

'Well... as it's Friday and the weekend now, and I'm virtually off duty, I guess a wine would be allowed,' she said grinning.

'I won't tell anyone, if you don't!' he said, passing her a large glass.

After a couple of refills, they were both feeling quite relaxed. 'May I ask you about your conviction? I mean—'

'Yes, what do you want to know?'

'What happened?'

'I got stitched up that's what happened. I would never, or could ever, view anything like that... but no-one believed me. I couldn't explain how it was on there, still can't,' he said looking down into his glass, swilling the last bit around. Knocking it back and getting up to open another bottle, he said, 'Apparently they had suspicions, so there was surveillance setup on my flat. They were able to show poor quality CCTV footage of me coming and going that apparently fitted in with the times the files were viewed, and that was the damning evidence, along with the files on my laptop of course. A living hell is all I can say, totally ruined my life. Well, up until I moved here and grew out my hair to change my appearance.'

'So you definitely didn't do it then?'

'I swear I didn't do it... on my life.'

Matthew's weeks settled into much the same fashion: work, visits to the takeaway and lots of watching TV. One evening, after a particularly stressful day dealing with overflowing toilets, he needed some fresh air. So after a quick supper, he headed out for a stroll before hitting the sack. With nowhere particular in mind, he headed towards the park and, enjoying the fresh air, carried on. Without taking much notice of the time, on a whim he suddenly thought he might pop in on James at his new apartment, give him a surprise.

Forgetting how long the trip across town took, he waited patiently for the next bus and hopped off it when he thought he must be near. Stopping a person to check he was going in the right direction, he turned the corner of James's road just as he could see some figures walking down some steps. Getting nearer, he could see one was James. But what he didn't expect to see was one of the police officers from his case. Watching from afar, two other figures then appeared and as the taxi pulled up, they all got in and sped away.

Wandering slowly back to the bus stop, he was a bit gutted that he hadn't timed his visit very well - a bit earlier and maybe he could have joined them. But he was also feeling hopeful -

maybe James was befriending the officer to help find out what had happened.

He thought about mentioning seeing James in a text to him, but then reconsidered. Expecting him to visit with some news very soon, a week later there was a knock on his door.

'Just popped in to see my little brother, check you are doing alright!' James said, giving him a hug and huge smile.

'Yep, ok thanks. How about you? What you been up to?' and grabbing them a beer each, they sat in the lounge while James gave the latest account of life in the 'stock market world.'

All the while he was listening with interest, he was eager to hear some other news. But as the conversation came to an end, and James got up to leave, nothing had been said.

'Just wondered... I know you said to leave the past in the past. But did you ever find anyone who might be able to look into my case?'

'Sorry Matthew, no... drawn a complete blank. But look, your life has moved on now hasn't it, so maybe we should just leave it.'

'But you must know someone. Don't you know anyone in the police, or know anyone who does?' waiting for him to say that maybe the officer wasn't able to help.

'God no! Our worlds don't mix - you know what our parties are like and some of the substances that are passed around. That would be a really bad idea, don't you think! Arrests on mass!' he said, nudging his arm.

But Matthew had seen them together.

That night, he couldn't sleep. Tossing and turning the whole time, he eventually got up feeling absolutely shattered. Why was his brother lying?

Getting another call from Monica, they arranged their next meeting.

He'd also hired a car and spent a few evenings watching outside James's apartment. One evening, after seeing the same police officer leave again, he followed him home - just so he knew where he lived. And just in case anyone still kept tabs on him, a different registration plate in the traffic would ensure everyone was none the wiser, particularly with his van still parked at home.

\* \* \*

On the quiet, Monica had also been asking some questions, which hadn't gone unnoticed.

'Who is this new probation officer Monica Turner? Anything I need to know?'

'I think her superior's words are 'young and keen, workaholic. She definitely wants to make a good impression, works all hours,' was the answer.

'She's just been asking about Matthew Watson's case, that's all. Make sure all the files are secure.'

'Already done.'

\* \* \*

Another late visit from Monica, and two bottles of wine, resulted in Matthew divulging what he'd seen. What had he got to lose?

'Can I tell you something confidential? Promise it won't be repeated outside of here?'

'Sure, go on. I'm intrigued now,' Monica answered, slurring slightly.

He then told her about seeing the police officer leaving his brother's apartment with him, and his brother lying about it afterwards.

'But did you ask him outright?'

'Didn't need to... I could tell he was lying. He forgets that being identical twins, I know him so well. While he has always lived the wild life, partying, drugs, lots of money, I have always been the one on the sidelines, watching. It's how I wanted it to be. I'm not jealous in the slightest, but it means I also *know* he was lying.'

'Why would he?'

'That bit I don't know.' The thought that he could have had anything to do with his arrest was now gnawing away at him.

'I have asked a few questions too you know, but got nowhere either,' she said.

'Wow, didn't expect you to say that. So you really do believe me then.'

'Told you I did... but it didn't help. Got sternly told *'the judge made his decision, your role is to try and ensure they don't end up in the courts again*!'

Walking her home later, to make sure she got there safely, he thanked her for a really lovely evening - but more importantly, for believing him. Neither noticed the occupants in a car parked outside of her flat taking photos.

Called into the office on Monday, Monica was given a formal final warning about her inappropriate behaviour. 'But we just bumped into each other and he walked me home, just to keep me safe. I mean, isn't that civilised behaviour from someone who is supposed to be a criminal!' she lied.

'You signed the professional code of conduct with your contract, you know the rules Monica!'

'And who the hell is spying on me?!' she exclaimed, seeing the photo on her superior's desk.

'Someone just noticed you, that's all. Anyway, because you are so good at your job, I've stuck up for you young lady. Matthew Watson will be appointed a new probation officer, so you can keep your job, but I can't and won't do this again and this conversation is now over, ok!'

There was no point in arguing and she really needed to keep her job. It was unnerving her though, that someone had been watching them.

She would find a way to keep in touch with Matthew even if she couldn't see him.

Outside of work, Matthew had been going out a lot more. A picture was beginning to emerge and not a good one. Each time, sat in a different hire car, he got to see the visitors to James' apartment and the police officer's home. And every time he slotted related questions into his conversations with James, James lied.

'Matthew, what's up?' seeing his brother's name appear on his phone.

'I'm really struggling James?' he quietly sobbed down the phone.

'Something happened?'

'Nothing particular, just think it's all caught up with me suddenly. Can I come over?'

'Um, er, yeah of course. I was expecting some visitors around later but no worries, I'll cancel them.'

'You sure? I don't want to put you out but could really do with having someone to talk to.'

'Give me an hour to do a quick phone around and get some supplies, see you at 6pm ok?'

'Thanks,' he murmured and hung up. Smiling, he was quite impressed with his acting skills for a change. James was always very cagey about meeting at his place, insisting they met at a bar or at his, so Matthew really hoped his plan would work - so far so good.

Compared to his pokey flat, James's new place was vast and very luxurious. Wandering over to get them both a drink, Matthew took a seat at the island in the kitchen before James showed him into the lounge. With massive sofas sat either side of a huge fireplace, they took a seat opposite each other in silence, sipping their drinks.

Keeping up the pretence, but also touched that his brother had quickly cancelled his plans to see him, Matthew was the first to speak.

'Means a lot, you dropping everything to see me.'

'I'm just pleased you turned to me for help – always said I'd be here didn't I. Felt really bad about before, but think you understand don't you?'

'Yeah I guess. So what were you supposed to be doing this evening?'

'Oh just a meet up with a regular group of friends - nothing that can't wait,' replied James. Seeing the obvious distress his little brother was in, he asked 'Are you working tomorrow?

'Day off actually, why?'

'Stay over tonight then. My spare room is always made up. I've got to be in a meeting by lunchtime so don't need to leave until mid morning, what do you say?'

'I'd love to, thanks.'

They spent the rest of the evening, drinking copious amounts of wine while reminiscing about the past. They agreed not to dwell on Matthew's time inside, instead steering the conversation away to more fun and mischievous times they'd had growing up. It felt like a lifetime since they'd done this and both fell into bed in the early hours feeling pretty drunk.

'Come on you, time to get up!' said James in his ear, with the music now blasting out from the kitchen.

'Oh god, I feel awful, think I'm going to be—' and Matthew flew out of the bed and dashed for the bathroom.

Hearing the awful noises coming from there, James called out, 'Want some headache tablets? Think it's about the only thing I've got in to help. I've made you a tea and bacon sandwich too!' but hearing more noises, headed off to his room to get dressed.

Knocking on the door of the bathroom, it was all quiet. 'Matthew, you ok?'

'Ugghhh. Yeah, I'll be alright once I stop throwing up,' he said groaning.

'Oh god. Well I've got to go now or I'll be late for my meeting. I'll leave you a key on the side - just post it back through the letterbox when you lock up, ok?'

'Thanks James, sorry about this.'

'Don't worry, I'll text you later just to check you've made it home ok. Bye!' and the door slammed shut.

Smiling to himself, it had worked.

Sitting in James's kitchen, drinking his tea and munching his bacon sandwich, he couldn't believe how well it had gone. James would never allow him a key at any of his places, and wouldn't ever give a reason why either. Used to make up stuff like, *'you'll probably lose it and then someone will break in,'* so it must have been an important meeting for him not to cancel it and wait for him to leave.

Quickly getting dressed, he snuck out the backdoor leaving it unlocked, and rushed down to the local Timpson to get a copy made. Within an hour, he was texting James to say thank you and that he was making his way home, so he could recover in his own bed.

'And the key?' came the reply.

'Posted back through the letterbox like you said. You can trust me ☺ Thanks for last night!'

'Pleased I could help you this time ☺.'

The next morning, the thud through the letterbox woke him up. Ripping the quilt back, he hurried to see what had made such a noise. Carefully opening the package, he was shocked to see a brick mobile phone, sim card and £10 'Pay as you go' voucher with a note.

*'Matthew,*

*Hope you're ok. Things have been a bit weird for me. Got called into the office and shown a photo of the two of us. Obviously this isn't allowed, so you will be hearing soon from your new probation officer. There's definitely something up, but need to keep my job. I want to keep in touch with you, so thought we could use these phones so we're not traced. Still want to support you though, so if you are free, meet me at the Palm House in Kew gardens at 4pm, M x'*

'Bloody hell, feels like something out of a Tom Cruise movie!' he muttered to himself, while quickly putting the phone on charge.

At 4pm she suddenly felt an arm put through hers. 'Good to see you,' he said quietly as they began wandering through the tropical garden, admiring all the plants.

'You too. Sorry if it seems a bit over the top, but got a bollocking at work for seeing you after hours and told in no uncertain terms, that our contact was to be over.'

'You mentioned a photo, could you tell where and when it was taken?'

'Yes - you dropping me back home.'

'What the hell? Look it's not worth causing you any grief honestly. Let's just forget about it.'

'I'm going to miss you though.'

'Yes, me too. How about we meet up like this for a bit? I've only got about six months of visits left, then we can see what happens from then, eh!' he said smiling at her and squeezing her hand.

Texting on their new phones, they kept in touch without anyone knowing.

Matthew also kept visiting James's apartment, convinced he would find something. James was so elusive and had started getting particularly shitty if Matthew mentioned joining him and his friends on their evenings at home.

'You'd hate it and you know nothing of our world... you'd be so out of your depth,' he would say.

'But it's not work is it? Thought it was a party. I can hold my own you know.'

'Get your own bloody friends Matthew!' and he hung up.

They'd always had different friends as adults, but he had never known him to be so adamant that Matthew would never be meeting this group.

One evening, he watched as a taxi pulled up and James flew down the steps and got in. Following them in his hire car, he watched him enter an exclusive property in one of the most expensive parts of the city. After waiting two hours, and with no-one else going in for the past hour, he decided to go home. 'Just an upper class dinner party probably,' he thought to himself.

But one fact was definitely emerging. It did appear that it was the same eight people who met up regularly.

Two weeks later, having seen the same small group arrive at James's the night before, he watched James leave to go to work and then dashed up the steps to let himself in.

Whilst everything looked ok, the lounge was laid out differently. A large projector screen was positioned above the fireplace and the seating rearranged to ensure everyone had a good view. Turning on the power, he took a seat while waiting for the screen to come alive. 'No signal found' appeared on the screen, so he hastily grabbed a couple of remote controls on the side and started pressing buttons.

'Jesus Christ, what were they watching?' he whispered, as an empty room with a bed appeared. Suddenly he could hear a key in the door and someone coming in. '*Shit*!' he frantically pressed all the power buttons and silently darted across the room to hide behind the large sideboard. Desperately trying to hold his breath, he watched James dash around looking for something. Stuffing his hand down the side of one of the cushions, he pulled out a wallet and, quickly putting it in his inside pocket, rushed out and slammed the door shut.

With his heart pounding, Matthew quietly let himself out and headed to the park for a bit of fresh air. On the off chance someone might be available, he sent a quick text. Two minutes later, the reply arrived, '*I'm due a break - St James' Park in thirty mins?*''

'*Fab, I'll grab us a coffee on the way!* ☺'

Hearing his findings at James's apartment, she shuddered at the thought. 'Did it give you any idea where the room could be?'

'No, could be anywhere.'

'Maybe you'll just have to be there one of the evenings... you know, out of sight. You've got a key now, so it is possible.'

'I know, but I'm still undecided as to whether I *want* to know. You know, I'm just trying to get my life back together now, this could scupper everything.'

'But can you carry on, knowing there could be something serious happening and you did nothing about it? And what if it had something to do with your case?'

'Oh cheers. Thanks for that,' he said nudging her arm, smiling at her. But they both knew he wouldn't be able to move on fully until he knew what was going on.

Two weeks later, having found out from James when he was next meeting up with his friends by asking about when they could have *their* next get-together, he was nervously waiting for the bus. Monica was the only who knew what he was doing.

'If I don't come back, you know where to look - especially if he suddenly gets a new patio!' he joked with her on text. He then promised he'd phone the minute he got back.

Making sure he was there in good time, well before anyone arrived, he looked around deciding it was too risky to be in the room, so the best place seemed to be the study just off the lounge. He could at least listen at the door. After going into the bathroom for a quick wee, he hid himself away awaiting the guests' arrival.

An hour later, having already heard James moving furniture around, there was a knock at the door and within minutes the apartment was filled with people clinking glasses and busily chatting. This went on for what seemed like ages, before James made an announcement for everyone to take their seats.

Standing at the study door, he could hear the whirr of the projector screen coming to life and then people starting to make their suggestions and demands: who, what and the price. As various acts began being played out live for them to watch, he could hear the cries of a young girl becoming increasingly distressed. With the realisation that James was fully involved, his immediate reaction was to burst into the room, shout at them all and call the police. But he also knew they were already there, well at least one of them. These were the sort of people that always knew people that could help so he would have to be cleverer than that. With his heart racing and desperate not to hear what was happening, he quietly crept to the other side of the room and clamped his hands tightly over his ears to shut it out.

At midnight, hearing the last person leave, he waited to hear James go into the bathroom and the shower come on, before he sped towards the door and out into the cold night air. Walking quickly towards the bus stop, the bus luckily arrived within a few minutes and he just stared out the window all the way home while trying to decide what to do. He had three texts from Monica, wondering what had happened, so the minute he was back in his flat, he got on the phone.

Shocked at his news, she was also worried for him. They arranged to meet up at his the following evening – she would sneak in once it was dark.

With a burst pipe that had flooded an office to keep him busy in the day, he'd had little time to dwell on the evening's events. Grabbing some filled rolls and cakes from the local bakery on the way home, he got in with just enough time for a quick shower before Monica was due.

She'd only been in the flat for about fifteen minutes when there was suddenly a knock at the door. Looking at each other, as he wasn't expecting anyone else, Matthew reluctantly decided to see who it was.

'James! Gosh, wasn't expecting you, everything ok?'

Walking straight into the lounge, he didn't wait for an invite. 'Oh, you have company, and you are...?'

'Hi, I'm Monica, nice to meet you,' she said standing up to shake his hand, feeling slightly flushed.

'You didn't tell me you had a girlfriend Matthew?'

'Uh, no - Monica is just a friend.'

'Well, lovely to meet you Monica. Anyway, just wondered if you fancied spending this weekend up at the cabin? It would be great for us to spend some time away together, like the good old days. It's been years since we were last up there together.'

'Right, ok. Um... sure. Would be fun I guess,' Matthew replied, a little flustered at not being able to think up of an excuse quickly.

'Good, I'll get all the supplies and meet you there - shall we aim to arrive about 7pm tomorrow then?'

'Sounds great, thanks.'

'Monica, you should come too?!' suggested James suddenly turning towards her.

'Oh I don't think so,'

'No, come on. It's lovely up there - we'll have a great time. A weekend away from everything, so good for all of us don't you think... proper time out?'

'Well I guess I could make it then, thank you.'

After quickly making the final arrangements and James confirming it was 'his treat, so no need to bring anything,' it was all agreed.

Monica still wasn't sure it was a good idea. 'I'm not supposed to be seen with you!'

'But no-one needs to know. I'll leave my van unlocked, you just get in. I'll let James know we'll be a bit late, so if we leave here at 7pm it will be dark and no-one will see. It will be fun, share with you the only good memories of when we were young. It'll be nice,' he said reassuringly.

The next morning, James called to double-check all was well with the arranged plans.

'You sure I can't bring anything?' asked Matthew.

'Nope, like I said my treat!'

With the revised time of arrival agreed, a very busy Friday flew past.

Setting off, Matthew was feeling anxious. Whilst he was looking forward to showing Monica the cabin and reminiscing about old times, he knew when he got back he had to do something about what was happening at James's. He and Monica had already chatted about phoning the police anonymously, *'a concerned member of the public has just heard a disturbance at the address, heard screaming,'* when the next get-together was taking place. 'That way they can't deny anything. And I'm really hoping it will also prove that James's involvement is minimal – maybe he's got himself in to something he can't get out of.'

Parking up at the cabin, the door flew open and James came down the steps to greet them. Hugging them both, he helped them in with their bags and showed them to their room. 'Don't worry, I've rearranged the beds and put two singles in there – know you said just friends, ok?!' he said grinning, with a twinkle in his eye.

'Thank you James,' replied Matthew smiling, as he and Monica plopped their bags on their beds.

Ten minutes later, they wandered into the lounge to a roaring fire and glasses of wine being handed to them. Collapsing onto the sofa, they both took a swig and let out a deep breath.

'Busy week? You both look shattered,' asked James, checking on the food in the oven.

'Yep, crazy busy. How about you?' replied Matthew.

'Same, very stressful... that's why I fancied popping out here for a change. No mobile phones to bother us either.'

Sitting at the table, they tucked into their food as they were ravenous.

'This is amazing, but you can't cook?!' exclaimed Matthew.

'I know, but I know lots of people don't I. Always someone to help me,' he said smiling at them both, while raising his glass to 'cheers' theirs.

After dinner, they took their drinks outside for a short while, until the midges started driving them mad. Sat in front of the fire, they both then began chatting about their holidays when they were young. Monica loved hearing them rib and laugh, reminding each other of all the things they got up to. Feeling the benefit of time out from city life, they then retired for the night.

'Can't believe he's involved really, can you?' Monica whispered from her bed.

'No. He has everything he could ever want, why would he want to be involved in that? Still, let's try and enjoy this weekend as it may not be happening again,' he whispered back.

Wandering into the kitchen the following morning, James was already up making coffee.

Passing them each a cup, he asked 'Can you both be ready by 11?'

'Of course, why... what have you got planned?' asked Matthew.

'Thought we all might like to go out on a boat – the weather is pretty good today, so wear your swim stuff! It should be here around 11am.'

'How exciting!' said Monica, taking her coffee back to their room to get ready.

A knock on the door and they were handed bacon rolls to have whilst they got up.

With just a gentle breeze, they took their seats and set off across the water. The sun was glistening on the lake and for a few hours it was just perfect. Their minds for now were happily distracted by the scenery that surrounded them. Coming to a stop, far out from the shore, the boat's engine was turned off.

'Who's going in first?!' James shouted, as he shoved a very unprepared Matthew off the side before joining him in the water.

Laughing, Monica dived off the boat and swam up to join them, shortly followed by James's friend Robert, who had agreed to be skipper for the day.

They all then headed for a large rock in the water, climbing out to sit in the sun for a few minutes before their swim back.

'Thanks for this,' said Matthew, feeling like old times with his big brother.

'Remember, we were never allowed this far were we, with the old battleaxe!' said James grinning.

'Good of her to leave us this place though, wasn't it! We've both had such good times here.'

'Yes, sure was.'

Getting back to the boat, Robert sailed them to a small cove around the corner for a spot of lunch.

Sat on the small sandy beach, wicker hamper contents spread out on a linen cloth, they supped the champagne and munched on the canapés, sharing stories and having such a great time... a world away from normal life.

Eventually this was interrupted by Robert, suggesting it might be a good idea to get back before dark and the arrival of all the midges again.

Feeling quite tipsy, they all took their seats and giggled as the boat sped them back to the cabin.

All jumping in the showers and getting changed before dinner, Monica suddenly grabbed Matthew and kissed him, something she had wanted to do for ages.

'We can't do this,' said Matthew, responding otherwise.

'I know, but out here no-one knows do they. Maybe one day I may have to think about a career change,' she whispered.

Half an hour later, they were all sat around the table, having their glasses filled with more wine. The curry that had arrived, from a restaurant thirty minutes away, was now sat in foil containers in the middle of the table, ready for everyone to help themselves.

'God I'm starving!' exclaimed Monica.

'Well, think I ordered enough... tuck in everyone!' announced James.

'Must have cost a fortune – thanks for organising this,' said Matthew.

'Said it was my treat this weekend, didn't I. And my world seems to be getting busier and busier, so wanted some time just for us.'

'Cheers everyone!' said Monica slurring slightly, standing up as she clinked her glass into theirs.

Sitting in the lounge after dinner, having another drink, James insisted he would tidy everything away and join them shortly.

Arriving to top up their glasses again, he noticed that Matthew and Monica were now starting to look quite drunk.

'You two ok?'

'It's just really gone to my head. Maybe I'm just not used to these expensive wines,' replied Matthew, looking at Monica.

'Yeah, me too. The ones I buy seem to be a lot weaker, can usually drink more than this,' said Monica, looking around as the room was slowly starting to spin. Starting to feel very strange, she took hold of Matthew's hand.

'You ok Monica, you don't look so good?' asked Matthew.

'It's just the room, it's starting to spin a bit. Maybe I shouldn't have any more to drink for a bit.'

Matthew put his arm around her as she was starting to look very unsteady.

'You sure you're allowed to do that?' said James smiling at them.

'What do you mean?' replied Matthew.

'Well, her being your probation officer and all that. Think it probably breaches the client/criminal protocol doesn't it?'

'I never told you she was a probation officer, how—'

Matthew's business card was suddenly flung out of James's pocket onto the coffee table in front of him.

'What's wrong?'

'Snooping on your own brother... found it under the curtain in my study!' he said suddenly very seriously.

'Must have dropped it when I stayed over at yours that day,' Matthew replied, trying not to panic.

'Don't lie Matthew, you were seen on CCTV!' he said angrily.

Finding Matthew's business card on the floor by the curtain in his study had changed everything. And when one of the group confirmed he had checked the CCTV back at the police station and watched Matthew enter James's home an hour or so before the group, and didn't leave until well after them, James knew there was no choice now.

'I told you to move on Matthew, why didn't you listen?'

Feeling something sting his neck, everything then suddenly went black.

Neither Matthew nor Monica had noticed Robert leave to go to the bathroom then quietly return and stand behind them, needle in hand.

With both of them already slipping into unconsciousness from the drugs James had added to their drinks, the effect from the injections was almost instant.

Putting them both in the back of Matthew's van, James and Robert got in and drove off quietly, with no lights on. Knowing these roads like the back of his hand was a definite advantage.

Pulling up at the cliff top, in a secluded part of the countryside, they stopped the van and got out.

Placing Matthew in the driving seat and Monica next to him in the front, James then pulled out a knife and plunged it into Monica's heart. Going back around to Matthew, he kissed his head and ruffled his hair. 'I'm so sorry Matthew, but had no choice - at least you can be together now,' and letting off the handbrake, closed the car door. Robert and James then slowly pushed the van off the cliff, watching it crash into the water below and disappear from sight.

Two weeks later, with reports from James that he couldn't get hold of him, the police broke into Matthew's flat. Finding no sign of him, they searched around trying to find clues as to what might have happened. Turning on his laptop they were horrified to find more images and videos. James hadn't been able to help them with their enquiries, apart from saying that Matthew had mentioned going to the cabin. Two days later they found the van and both bodies. Forensics confirmed that the knife was from his flat and their DNA was found on wine glasses in the cabin. With no witnesses and the limited evidence they had found, the conclusion was that Monica must have somehow seen the laptop and confronted Matthew. Being so traumatised from his sentence before, Matthew couldn't face being sent to prison again - he wouldn't have coped. Neighbours confirmed they had seen Monica at the flat a few times.

Murder-suicide was the verdict - so sad, just like his mum and dad.

And as the case hit the headlines, conversations were sparked around the country - with chat shows, psychologists and radio stations discussing the 'nature/nurture' debate once again.

A week after the cremation service, James collected Matthew's ashes to take him on his final journey. Sitting at the end of the jetty, back at the cabin, he said a few words.

'I really *am* sorry for how things turned out Matthew. But when one of our girls recognised me from a TV interview I had done for work, I had to act quickly - you must understand. Lucky for me we look so similar and buying the same high street clothes as you was a doddle. And of course knowing the right people in the right places, tracks were quickly altered. I've learnt to be more careful, so less hands-on now. I know some people say we go somewhere from here, so if we do, you are now with someone you couldn't really be with in this world. See... told you I think of you,' and tipping the urn upside down, Matthew's ashes were released into the breeze, landing on the water and then disappearing under the surface.

Standing back up, James muttered, 'Anyway, must dash. People to see, deals to be done.'

# The Note That Changed Everything

'Come in!' Mr Watson called out, hearing a knock on the door.

'Sir, Mrs Cole says can you cover Mr Williams' after-school club? He's had to go home.'

'Um, yes of course. Tell her no problem, thank you Emily.'

'Connor, grab your stuff. You'll have to come with me.'

With a big sigh, Connor reluctantly followed Mr Watson down the corridor to the drama hall.

'Right, you can sit at the table over there and carry on with your work, ok?'

Without answering, Connor dumped his bag by the table and took a seat.

'Good afternoon everyone. Mr Williams can't make it today, so I'm covering. Can someone tell me what piece we are practising at the moment?'

'Hall of the Mountain King sir.'

'Ok – let's get started then. Woodwind instruments, can you start playing first please,' and as the flutes, clarinets and oboes began playing, he lifted his baton and started directing them from the sheet music on the stand in front of him.

'Ooh. Stop everyone, just flutes this time. There's something slightly amiss there.'

And as the flutes section began playing the first part of the music on their own, Connor sat back in his chair staring at them all.

Noticing the lack of work being done, as the music stopped Mr Watson turned to Connor. 'This isn't an excuse to sit and do nothing.'

'How am I supposed to concentrate with all this bloody noise?!'

'Connor!' Mr Watson shouted back at him. 'I will not have you swearing in school, who the hell do you think you are?! You've just added another two weeks to your detention time with me, during and after school, well done!'

As some of the orchestra giggled, Connor slammed his hand down on the table. 'You can't make me if I'm not in *bloody* school!' and with that he grabbed his bag and ran to the door.

'Connor!' but he'd gone.

Down at the shops, he was handed a smoke. 'Don't know why you bother going anyway? Waste of bloody time.'

'I know, but mum gets really upset. She was in tears again the other night so I promised her I'd go.'

'Well, up to you mate but I wouldn't bother.'

'Oi Ryan, wait up!' and they all hurried to catch up with Ryan.

Congregated in a large group outside the local shops, an evening of hanging around intimidating people and egging each other on to nick stuff followed. With the local newsagent getting a barrage of abuse, whilst some of his stock was stuffed into jacket pockets, they larked around without a care for anyone.

But two evenings later, returning for much of the same, they hadn't expected to be greeted with a baseball bat.

'Get the hell away from my shop!' the shopkeeper yelled at them, swinging it around to try and ward them off.

'You can't do that old man!' Ryan told him, getting closer and closer to him.

'Keep away!' he replied, with the baseball bat skimming Ryan's coat.

'Now that was stupid!'

Ryan ripped the bat out of his hand and swung it around, crashing it down on the back of the old shopkeeper's head. As he dropped to the floor, Ryan laughed. 'Come on lads, best get going!' and they fled into the local estate.

Hearing the sirens ten minutes later, they all drifted their separate ways. 'Not a word!' Ryan warned them all as they parted company.

An hour later, the police were at Connor's flat questioning him.

'So you've no idea why someone would say it was you then?'

'No. You've got to believe me.'

'Were you there? Did you see anything?'

Connor just looked down at the floor.

'We know Ryan Brown had something to do with it Connor, just tell us.'

But he knew he couldn't say anything.

'Connor, tell them what you know,' his mum implored him. 'I don't know what to do anymore,' she said, turning to both police officers.

They both knew that Connor was probably being stitched up, being the newest member of this gang. 'Well, we'd better get going. We'll be carrying on with our enquiries and will probably come and talk again soon. So I'd keep your head down for a bit Connor – maybe try and go to school a bit more often too.' Seeing the disappointment on his mum's face, one of the officers turned to her. 'We checked in with the school about a number of the lads hanging around here, just to see if they could shed any light on anything. Think you may be hearing from them about Connor's attendance very soon.'

Closing the front door, having told the officers that they were welcome to come back anytime, she couldn't hide her upset.

'I am sorry Mum.'

'No you're not, or you wouldn't do it. Empty words Connor, I've heard them too often recently. You'll end up with nothing you know – and don't think they're your friends either. Friends don't act like they do.'

'But Mum...'

But she wasn't listening now, she was too sad. Closing her bedroom door, she collapsed onto her bed and took hold of the photo frame with a two year old Connor grinning back at her, looking so cheeky and adorable. Hugging it to her chest, she let the tears spill down her cheeks. Half an hour later, having splashed some water on her face and taken a deep breath, she opened the door to the lounge. Without saying anything she took a seat next to him and took hold of his hand. 'Please just tell me you didn't hurt that old man?'

'I didn't Mum, I promise.'

Waking up to hear Mum in the kitchen with the radio on, Connor double-checked that it wasn't Saturday. Nope, it was definitely Monday.

Washed, dressed and bag packed, he arrived in the kitchen to the smell of bacon sandwiches.

'I wasn't sure if you were thinking about going to school today, so I thought I'd come with you!' she announced.

'Mum – you can't!'

'Watch me!' she answered with a smile that told him she absolutely was.

Walking through the school gates, he couldn't wait for her to leave. But his mum had other plans.

'No, we're going to the office together.'

With Connor cringing with embarrassment, they were both asked to take a seat while the receptionist tracked down the headteacher.

Ten minutes later, they were being welcomed into her office.

'Thank you for coming to see us Mrs Taylor. Good to see you too Connor.' And thirty minutes later, a plan was agreed. One that Connor had no choice in.

'This is your last chance Connor.'

'I don't like it anymore than you Connor, so stop feeling sorry for yourself,' Mr Watson told him as he'd arrived at his classroom after the bell for first break.

'How come you have to do this then sir?'

'That doesn't concern you. Anyway, I'm going to grab a coffee and then I'll be right back. Don't go anywhere!'

Taking a seat at one of the desks, Connor sat looking out at everyone messing about in the playground. He often found it pretty boring out there anyway, unless there was a football to kick about.

'Right, you can help me sort all this paperwork out,' announced Mr Watson, dumping down a load of photocopied material on the table. After telling him what was what, Mr Watson sat and drank his coffee while Connor sorted the various papers into piles.

With the bell then signalling that break was over, Mr Watson informed him where he would meet him at lunchtime.

Opening their packed lunch boxes, they sat opposite each other in the empty classroom. 'Why do you act up like you do Connor? You're a bright lad,' Mr Watson asked him, interrupting the silence.

'Dunno sir.'

'But you do know, you're not stupid. You also know, that at the end of the day, the only person that this will really damage is you, don't you?' Having waited for a response, he added, 'Well, you've only got this year left of school, so don't mess it up is my only advice, whether you take it or not. You really will regret it one day.'

That evening, laid on his bed, he thought about what Mr Watson had said. But he also thought about the area they lived in and what chances there were for his future, they all seemed pretty shit as far as he could see.

If he wasn't in a gang, he was their target – no thanks.

If he didn't involve himself and do what they said, at least to a limited degree, things soon turned violent. He didn't fancy a repeat of the kicking he got one night after refusing to join in robbing two young lads, who were just innocently walking home.

And work options in the local area were dire.

So all told, school was a waste of time and everything was absolutely shit.

But a knock on his door, jolted him out of these thoughts. 'Yep.'

'I didn't wake you did I? It's just I need to pop down the shops and wouldn't mind some company. I never feel that safe – not now anyway.'

''Course mum. Wait a sec while I get my trainers on.'

'Evening Mrs Taylor,' three lads called out as they passed them. 'Coming out later Connor?'

'Nah, not tonight,' said Connor as he hastily entered the shop with his mum.

'That lot have been hanging around causing mischief all evening,' the shopkeeper told them, as he was scanning the shopping in their basket.

'Connor knows them, he'll have a word with them. Won't you Connor.'

'They won't listen to me mum,' said Connor, then looking at the shopkeeper he added, 'Sorry.'

'Ah don't worry Connor. Just don't become like them eh! The only place that lot are going to end up is prison or the cemetery.'

'And you know he's right,' said his mum, as they left the shop to walk home.

'Right Connor, help me with this will you?' asked Mr Watson, handing him a laminating machine to carry into a classroom while he lugged a box of papers.

Plugging it in, he said, 'Ever used one?'

'No sir.'

'Well, we've been volunteered to make up the tickets for the junior school concert in a few weeks time. All this lot have got to be laminated and then chopped up, using the guillotine. So unless you've got homework to catch up on, I thought you'd give me a hand,' he said, lifting out a large pile of A4 paper, printed with all the concert details on.

Nearly an hour later, with the bell signalling the lunch hour was over, they shoved everything in a cupboard to finish the next day. 'How about we meet here at break tomorrow to finish them off?' said Mr Watson.

'Ok sir. See you then,' replied Connor as he headed off to his afternoon classes.

*The Note That Changed Everything*

Whilst they had hoped to finish at morning break the next day, they hadn't anticipated how long it would actually take, so agreed to carry on again at lunchtime. But walking up to the door at 12.15pm, he could see an envelope pinned to the outside with his name on.

'Connor, I've got to cover a club so have moved our stuff over there. Please come to Music Room 3, Mr Watson.'

Arriving to hear a few instruments tuning up, Connor took a seat at the back of the room whilst Mr Watson chatted with the few players about what songs they were learning.

'Where's Zack? Has anyone seen him?'

'No sir.'

'Oh. Well we need someone on drums, any volunteers?'

Silence.

'Connor, ever played drums before?'

With a horrified look on his face, he looked up and shook his head.

'Uh, no sir.'

'Fancy a go?'

'No sir.'

'Wrong answer, come and have a go.'

'But I don't know what I'm doing.'

'You'll learn.'

Half an hour later, 'Seven Nation Army' was sounding pretty similar to The White Stripe's version. As the bell rang, everyone downed instruments and hastily began packing away. The time had flown past, a thoroughly enjoyable time for everyone – including Mr Watson and Connor.

'You're pretty good you know,' said Matt, as he put his guitar back in its case.

'Thanks. You guys are so good, you should think about playing somewhere sometime,' said Connor.

*The Note That Changed Everything*

'Cheers mate.'

Later that day, sat at the small table in their kitchen, Connor mentioned the music session to his mum.

'I knew something had happened today, and something good for a change. You look different – happier. Can you go again?'

'Doubt it, remember I'm with Mr Watson every break. And it was only because he was covering and the drummer was off school. Anyway, doesn't matter.'

But Mr Watson had also noticed the sudden difference in Connor. Like a light had been switched on.

With half term around the corner, Mr Watson was checking in with Connor before the holidays.

'Don't get into any trouble ok. Think of your mum, but also think about you and your future. Have some lie-ins, play your Xbox all day if it keeps you busy and out of other people's way! And we both know who we are talking about, don't we.'

'Easier said than done sometimes though sir.'

'I know,' replied Mr Watson, lightly patting him on the back.

Popping down the local shop to get his mum some milk, there they were. *Shit.*

'Oi Connor, where you been?' shouted Ryan.

'Busy mate,' Connor said hurrying into the shop.

'So have we,' said Ryan, catching up with him and showing him the wad of notes in his pocket.

Grabbing a bar of chocolate off the shelf, he ripped it open and began eating it.

'Coming out tonight, you swot?!' he said, nudging Connor's arm. 'School ain't no excuse now is it.'

'Um, maybe,' and he swiftly headed for the till.

'That's £1.50 please,' and as he handed the shopkeeper the money, Ryan chucked his empty wrapper at the man and sauntered out the door.

Handing him his change, Connor said, 'Here's £1.00 for his chocolate bar, sorry.'

'You don't need to pay for him Connor.'

'I know, but please take it.'

'Thank you – you're a good lad.'


With his mum out busy working, Connor was trying to lie low. Having cleaned and tidied their flat, he lay on his bed with his earphones in and drifted off listening to music. He hadn't heard his mum getting home until there was a knock at his door.

'Oh hi Mum, you're early,' he said, looking at the clock.

'Yes,' she said smiling. 'The offices weren't as bad as normal, we had it all cleaned in record time today, so finished early. And look what I picked up on the way home,' she said holding up a bag from the local chip shop.

'Fancy eating our sausage and chips in front of the TV?'

'Yeah,' he said, getting up from his bed.

But just as Connor was getting the ketchup out of the fridge there was an unexpected knock at the door.

Opening it, there stood Ryan and a couple of the others.

'Your phone not working Connor mate?'

Just as he was about to answer, his mum said, 'Actually Ryan, I'd rather you didn't come around here anymore.'

'Why's that then Mrs Taylor?' Ryan said, in a slightly intimidating manner, leaning on the doorframe.

*The Note That Changed Everything*

'It's alright mum, I'll pop outside to talk to Ryan.'

'Don't be long though Connor,' she said, putting their food in the oven to keep warm.

But hearing Ryan's latest idea filled Connor with horror. 'No way, you've got to be *bloody* joking.'

'It's not much, maybe half a kilo. And it won't be for long, I've got it for someone who'll get the money to me in a week or so. You just need to stash it for me until then.'

'I can't.'

'You can and you will,' he told him, as Connor walked back up to their flat.

'What did he want?' his mum asked, the minute he stepped foot in the lounge.

'Um, nothing much.'

'Don't let Ryan ruin your future. He'd throw you under the bus soon as look at you, and don't kid yourself that he wouldn't.'

'You don't understand mum.'

'Try me,' she said, patting the seat next to her. 'I wasn't born yesterday.'


Connor arrived back at school in a lighter mood. And Mr Watson was the first to notice.

'Welcome back Connor – good break?'

'Yes it was ok sir. Laid low like you said to,' he replied smiling, which was a rare thing at school.

'Good, good. Oh by the way, I've been asked to cover the lunchtime band club for the rest of the year, so every Wednesday and Friday we'll be in Music Room 3, ok?

'Sure.'

Trying to concentrate on his work was nearly impossible, being distracted with the band playing.

*The Note That Changed Everything*

'Fancy trying bass guitar Connor?'
'Wh-what?'
'Bass guitar... come and have a go,' said Mr Watson.
'But I've no clue.'
'Jack will help you, won't you Jack?'
'Sure.'

Sending them to the back of the room, Mr Watson carried on with Matt on lead guitar and Zach on drums, while Jack helped Connor learn the chords he needed for the song they were practising. And no-one was more surprised than Connor, when it just seemed to click.

'Wish I'd learnt that quick,' said Jack as they rejoined the group.

Two sessions later, they were getting pretty good at playing 'Smells like Teen Spirit.'

But that Sunday, sat watching TV with his mum in the lounge, their quiet evening was suddenly interrupted by pounding on the door and the words 'Police, open the door!' being shouted.

Rushing up to open the door, the police charged past them and began searching their flat for drugs. Connor's name had been mentioned.

'You've got the wrong place!' his mum shouted at them, as they began turfing drawers out onto the floor and tipping over their beds. 'Why don't you try Ryan's house!'

'We have already.'

Finding nothing, the police apologised before leaving Connor and his mum to clear up the mess.

Closing the door Connor looked at his mum. 'Where did you put it?' he mouthed.

'I sorted it, I said I would.'

'You didn't get rid of it, did you?' he pleaded. 'I'll be dead.'

'Of course not, it's in my cleaning trolley at work.'

'Oh mum,' he said, hugging her tight.

That night, lying in bed, her mind was filled with how she had to get them off the estate. She would contact head office and see about getting some more hours.

On the way to school the next morning, Ryan was waiting for him.

'Heard you had a visit last night.'

'Yep,' replied Connor, walking as fast as he could without looking odd.

'Still got it.'

'Yep.'

'Good,' and he walked off in the other direction.

Band practice that week was a welcome distraction, and an escape from thinking about everything else. But Mr Watson had noticed that something was up.

'Care to share anything?' he asked Connor, as they were the last to leave the room on the Friday.

'No.'

'Are you sure?'

'Just stuff sir.'

'Ok, well if you want to talk, I'm all ears. Oh, before we go, take this home with you,' and he handed him a guitar case. 'Practice over the weekend and bring it back with you on Monday, ok?'

'Thanks sir.'

Getting in the door from work that evening to hear Connor playing along to some music, his mum dropped her bag on the floor and took a seat on the sofa. Ten minutes later, noticing the time, he opened his bedroom door to find his mum sat listening.

'That was so good Connor, maybe you'll need to find a band to play with one day,' she said, bursting with pride.

The following day, doing some shopping in town, they both stopped as they heard a band playing in the distance. Changing direction to follow the music, they found Zach, Jack and Matt busking near the subway with quite a crowd now gathered to listen.

'That's who I practice with at school mum – good aren't they?'

'Amazing.'

As the band finished another song, coins were dropped into their guitar case as Connor and his mum wandered off again unnoticed to finish their shopping.

'You should join them next time?'

'Oh they won't want me. I only play with them because I have to be with Mr Watson.'

Handing the guitar back on Monday, he thanked Mr Watson who then asked him to play what he'd been practising.

'Sorry I don't recognise that last bit, what song is that from?'

'Oh I made that bit up.'

'Really? Well you obviously have a gift,' he told him, as Connor placed the guitar back in its case and handed it to him.

And while over the weekend Connor had practised and practised, playing along to tracks on his phone, his mum had been wracking her brain as to how she was going to change

*The Note That Changed Everything*

their life. While they lived where they did, Connor didn't stand a chance.

Having phoned head office, as well as asking around at work, she learned there was sadly no more hours available and they couldn't offer her anything else. Also, relying on buses to get around meant her area was restricted, so while she loved her neighbours and friends, she decided there was little choice but to think about moving away.

'Don't be daft mum, this is all you know!' said Connor, hearing her idea.

'But you are more important. I couldn't bear it if anything happened to you.'

'I'll be ok mum.'

A sudden bitterly cold snap meant the estate went unusually quiet, which was very welcome. It was only on the Friday, on her way home from work, that Connor's mum spotted a sign outside their local pub saying, 'Live Music tonight at 8pm – everyone welcome!'

'There's a band playing at the Royal Oak this evening, fancy going?' she asked Connor as soon as she got in the door.

'Yeah, that'd be nice.'

Half an hour later, they were leaving the flat and heading out into the cold. Squeezing through the packed pub, she managed to get them a coke each and get back to her seat, just as the band began playing.

'Who knew we had such a brilliant band on our doorstep!' she said a couple of hours later, tucking her arm into his as they left to walk home.

'Thanks for a great evening mum, I've loved it.'

But as they arrived back home, Ryan was stood there waiting.

'Think you've something of mine that I need back now, Connor.'

'Um, yeah, ok. Wait a minute.'

Getting in their flat, he was panicking. 'Mum, where is it?'

'Oh god, it's still at work.'

'We've got to get it mum!'

'I don't know if I can get in. Security may not let me in out of hours.'

'Gonna have to try – I'll come with you.'

Closing the door, Connor updated Ryan.

'After the police raid I had to move it, didn't I? I'm not frigging stupid you know!'

'How long will you be?'

'Dunno. Probably an hour or two,' and he pushed past him with his mum to head to the bus stop.

Sitting on the bus, willing it to go faster, they finally reached the office block.

'Hi Gus, I know it's late but is it alright if I quickly pop up and get something I left behind in my locker?' she asked the security guard, sat behind the reception desk.

'Well, we're not supposed to... but I guess as it's you Mandy, sure,' and he buzzed her through. Pressing the button in the lift, they travelled up in silence. Getting out at floor 10, Connor followed her along the corridor until they reached the cleaning room.

'Wait here,' she whispered as she swiped her lanyard and disappeared behind the door.

Rummaging through her trolley, she popped the package in her bag and headed back out.

'Bye then Gus, see you Monday,' she called out as they passed through reception and left the building.

And it was no surprise that Ryan had been waiting for their return. Passing Ryan the package, he handed Connor some cash. 'Told you it would be worth your while.'

'And he's not doing it again Ryan,' Mandy said sternly as she put the key in the lock.

'We'll see,' Ryan answered as he walked off.

At work, with barely anyone left on the office floor, Mandy was busy cleaning when she spotted Chris, one of the senior managers, in his office on the phone. She watched as he slammed the phone down, muttered a few curse words and put his head in his hands, looking completely exasperated. Five minutes later, his office door opened.

'Oh sorry Mandy, didn't realise you were still here?'

'Should be out of your way soon,' she replied.

'Oh no rush, I'm off now anyway. See you tomorrow,' and he left.

Wandering into his office, she emptied the bin and was about to start dusting when she noticed a post-it note left by his phone: 'Home from Home care' £1500pw, Care Angels £1800pw, Daffodil care services £1600pw.

'Bloody hell, who can afford that?' she muttered to herself, as she ran the duster over his desk and left the room.

Arriving home after a tiring shift, she put the kettle on and knocked on Connor's door.

'You ok, how was your day?' she asked him before realising he still had his earphones in.

'Oh hi mum, you ok?'

'Yes thanks, I was just asking you the same.'

*The Note That Changed Everything*

'Yeah ok I suppose. Got some of my mock marks today and maths is bad, fancy helping me?'

'Oh god, I'm useless at maths. George, four doors down, used to work at the bank. I'm sure he'd love to help you. Tell you what, I'll pop down and ask him while the tea is brewing.'

Coming back in the door, Connor had finished making their tea and was sat waiting in the lounge.

'Yes, he said he'd be delighted to help you. But he also chuckled saying he hoped *it hadn't gone all modern*! I said you'd go and see him after school tomorrow, ok?'

'Cool.'

Between school, Mr Watson and now George, there was little time for anything else. On the rare occasion it was free, Mr Watson also leant him a guitar to practise on. Then wandering past Cash Converters on the way home from school one afternoon, Connor spotted a bass guitar in the window so popped inside to find out more. Taking it down from the window and handing it to him, the shop assistant found him a chair to sit on and try it out. Customers perusing the many items for sale, all began turning around hearing him play.

'You ought to play in town you know. Could earn yourself a bit playing like that,' said one of them.

'Thanks,' he said blushing slightly at the attention.

'And sorry, how much is it?'

'£110 for that one.'

'Oh. You wouldn't accept £100 would you? It's all I've got.'

'Sorry we can't.'

*The Note That Changed Everything*

'Here you go,' said an elderly lady, smiling. 'You have a talent you know, I'll gladly give you the extra £10. You must buy it.' And seeing the look on his face, she added, 'Please.'

'Thank you so much. You have no idea how much this means to me, thank you.'

'Enjoy it my love,' and handing him a £10 note she left the shop.

Getting back home, he couldn't really believe what had happened. Sat in the lounge playing as his mum walked through the door, she took a seat to listen.

'How did you get that?'

'The £100 Ryan gave me, for... you know.'

'Promise me though it won't happen again. Don't get lulled or tempted into anything to do with him.'

'Promise.'

While Connor was studying like crazy for his exams, Mandy knew it wouldn't be long before Ryan would be back. They had to get out of there somehow. Gangs were taking over the area more and more, and she worried so much about how she could protect Connor from getting caught up in it. Some days it seemed impossible.

With her change in demeanour, like she had the world on her shoulders, she was vacuuming the main floor when she bumped into Chris coming out of his office. 'Oops, sorry!'

'No problem.' And then seeing the tears in her eyes, he asked, 'You ok Mandy? Come and take a seat in my office.'

She insisted she was fine and just being silly, but he wouldn't take no for an answer.

Sat at the other side of his desk, and handed a cup of coffee from the vending machine, he asked, 'What's up?'

'Oh nothing really.'

Still staring at her, waiting for a proper answer, he said nothing.

'Oh, just kids you know. Do you have any?'

'Yes. A boy and a girl.'

'So you know how much we worry sometimes then?'

'Oh yes, but you've worked here for years and I've never seen you like this. You can talk to me you know.'

'Oh, just some gangs hanging around our estate. I'm worried my son may get caught up in something he can't get out of.'

'Have you thought about moving?'

'On my wages, you're joking. Sorry, didn't mean for it to come out like that, I'm grateful for this job honestly. But housing is so expensive, I can't find anywhere else I can afford.'

'Have you thought about getting another job maybe? I mean, I don't want you to leave or anything, but have you asked head office about more hours or anything?'

'Yes, but apparently there's nothing more they can give me. I've looked around at other jobs but there really isn't anything at the moment.'

'Hmm. Well, if I think or hear of anything I'll let you know.'

'Thanks... and thanks for listening.'

'Anytime,' and she left to get back to her cleaning.

The following week, entering the cleaning room to grab her trolley, there was a handwritten envelope on top: Private & Confidential: Mandy.

'Oh no,' she gasped, fearful at what could be inside. Maybe her coming in late that evening, maybe someone had seen her leave early that day... but no, it said: 'Dear Mandy,

I've been thinking about our chat. Can you let me know when you are free on a weekday morning and pop it on a note on my desk. I would like to see you about something private, thanks Chris.'

'Ooh intriguing,' she smiled to herself, as she scribbled down some days and times.

The next evening she arrived to find another note: 'Great, meet me outside the office at 10.30am on Tuesday, Chris. PS. It's nothing to do with here so please keep it to yourself.'

Connor was as intrigued as his mum.

'So what could it be? Any idea?'

'Not really. Maybe he wants a private cleaner for his house or something.'

Tuesday morning arrived and hearing a car beep, she smiled and got in.

'Morning Chris.'

'Morning, well I guess you are wondering what on earth this is all about? I couldn't talk about it at work but would like you to come and meet my mum.'

'Sorry, what?'

'I know it seems a bit random, but our conversation got me thinking. My mum is starting to need more help now and we always promised we wouldn't put her in a home. My wife and I both work full-time and neither of us can afford to jack in our jobs to look after her. Care agency fees are just ridiculous and so unaffordable, so we thought maybe if we got someone to move in and live with her. And I've known you a long time, so thought if you came and met her, and you liked each other, that that may be an option that could suit everyone. What do you think?'

'Um, er... I'm a bit taken aback to be honest.'

'Please don't say no yet. Come and see her for a cup of tea and take a look around, and then decide.'

'Ok,' she replied, feeling slightly hesitant but also a bit excited.

Pulling up outside a large terraced Victorian house in Maida Vale, she gasped. 'She lives here?'

'I know, it's a bit big isn't it. But she's never lived anywhere else.'

Opening the front door, he called out, 'Mum, it's Chris. I've brought Mandy to come and see you, ok if we come in?'

'Of course dear,' a voice called out and they entered the lounge to find his mum sat watching the TV. Clicking the off button she said, 'Hello Chris dear, and hello to you Mandy dear, do come and take a seat.' Patting the sofa next to her, Mandy went and sat down.

'Mandy, this is my mum Anna. I'll just go and get us some tea,' and Chris left them to it.

Ten minutes later, holding a tray of tea and biscuits, he arrived to find them happily chatting on the sofa. Mandy had picked up some of the photos from the sideboard, with Anna now pointing out and explaining who was who. She'd also found some old photos of Chris as a teenager.

'Oh mum, we don't want to put her off, thanks for that!'

Chatting over tea about the help Anna needed, Mandy tried to contain her excitement. This could be just the fresh start she and Connor needed. 'And I guess I should show you around, shouldn't I?'

'Sure,' said Mandy, getting up from the sofa.

The house was simply beautiful, and such a calm space. Going in and out of the rooms, she felt like pinching herself. But she knew Anna had to like her and want her there, it wouldn't work otherwise.

Arriving back in the lounge, Anna was gazing out of the window at the trees. 'So what do you think Mandy dear? Do you think you could cope living here and helping me?'

'Oh gosh, I would love to. It would be an honour. But I have a son too; he would need to come with me.'

'Of course dear. It would be lovely to have a youngster around again, I absolutely love it when the grandchildren pop in to see me. How old is he?'

'15.'

'Do you think he would like it here?'

'Oh yes,' especially since she had seen the music room at the back of the house. *Connor would be beside himself if he was here now,* she thought to herself. There was so much space; the bedrooms were virtually the size of their whole flat.

'Well you and Chris have a chat away from here and make the decision. But from me, I think it could work really well – you are a lovely person, I can just tell.'

Giving Anna a small hug goodbye, Chris then bent down to kiss his mum on the cheek. 'I've got today off mum, so I'll pop back again once I've dropped Mandy home.'

'Ok dear.'

Locking the door, they walked down the front steps to the car in silence. Setting off, Chris said, 'Well I guess we should talk about money. You obviously wouldn't have any bills or rent to pay, food is included too, so we were hoping £300 per week would be acceptable. My wife and I will give you time off every other weekend. So what do you think?'

'Oh my god, this is like my prayers have been answered. I would absolutely love to look after your mum Chris, I can't thank you enough.'

'You just have by saying yes. We have been at our wits end, fretting with what's going to happen, wait until I tell my wife!' and with that, he dialled her mobile on loud speaker and the car was filled with whoops of joy.

After visiting with Connor, for him to meet Anna and all the family, the final arrangements were then made. Connor only needed to go in for exams now, so whilst the bus would take well over an hour, it was only short-term so definitely worth it. And while Mandy and Connor got busy sorting and packing up their home, excited families from the council house waiting list were being contacted about viewing their flat.

And no-one was more pleased for Connor than Mr Watson.

'About time some luck came your way,' he told him hearing the news. 'I expect your mum is chuffed and relieved at the same time.' Connor nodded.

'By the way, did you hear that Jack's band have been given a slot at a local band night? I reckon you should ask them if you could be a part of it too.'

'No, that's ok sir. I might go and watch them though, if I can.'

But leaving school that day, he was soon joined by Ryan. 'You changed your number or something?'

'Um, no.'

'Well bloody well answer it then.'

'Go away Ryan.'

But Ryan wasn't going anywhere. Getting him by the scruff of the neck, he shoved him up against the wall. 'Don't you go getting bloody smart with me Connor, who the fuck do you think you are talking to?'

*The Note That Changed Everything*

Connor struggled, looking down at the floor. 'Oi, leave him alone!' called out the shopkeeper that had just come out the back to put some cardboard in the bin.

'I've got another package for you to look after, I'll be in touch,' and Ryan let go of him and hastily walked off.

'You ok Connor?' asked the shopkeeper, arriving at his side.

'Yes thanks,' even though he really wasn't.

What was he going to do? His mum couldn't risk taking it to work again, and this could ruin their plans - if Chris and his family found out they would never let them go and live with Anna.

Dreading a knock at the door and a visit from Ryan, Connor didn't let on to his mum about their last conversation. Desperate to keep out of everyone's way, apart from going to school, he barely left the flat. However as dates were agreed and the time drew nearer to them moving, Ryan still hadn't turned up, which was strange. It was only early one morning, dashing down to the local shop to put some money on the gas meter, that he learnt that Ryan had been remanded in custody on assault charges. He just prayed it was for long enough.

Six weeks later they were locking the door for the last time and handing over the keys. Mandy had worked her notice and said her final goodbyes to the office and her neighbours. And whilst she said she'd pop back sometime if she could, they all knew they probably wouldn't see each other again. And no-one was more shocked than Ryan, when three months later having served his short prison sentence, he knocked on their door only to find new residents in their flat.

Having knocked loudly five times, he wasn't expecting the door to be opened by a six foot, seventeen stone bloke in his mid-thirties. He could also hear a baby crying in the background.

'Cheers for waking us all up!' he said sternly to Ryan. 'What do you want?!

'Um... is Connor there?'

'No.'

'Do you know where he's gone?'

'No, now piss off!' he said, having taken an instant dislike to Ryan.

'Uh, sorry,' and Ryan headed for the stairs.

Asking around, heads shook - no-one knew where they'd gone.

It didn't take long for Mandy and Connor to settle into life at Anna's, all feeling very content in each other's company. Anna adored having them live in the house, and even more so the first time Connor played the guitar for her. Making him promise to make the music room his space, she just asked for one of her chairs to be put in there for her to take a seat occasionally.

Connor did well enough in his exams to gain an apprenticeship working on a local building site, however after a couple of years decided it wasn't for him after all, so ended up getting a job behind the bar in a local pub.

One Saturday evening, he was busy serving a packed bar waiting for the live music to start, when he heard raised voices.

'You're joking... look how many have turned up! You could have let me know sooner Josh!' said Dave, the landlord.

'I've only just bloody well found out myself!' answered Josh.

'Connor – you play bass don't you?' asked Dave, turning to look at him.

'Um, yeah... but only for a bit of fun.'

'Would you help us out, just for tonight?' asked Josh, imploring him to say yes.

''Course he will, won't you Connor. You've still got time to get ready, you're not due on for another thirty minutes yet.'

Apart from the few times he'd plucked up the courage to do some busking locally, he'd never played outside of the house. He wondered whether his nerves would get the better of him, so excused himself to make a quick phone call.

'Hello Connor dear, everything ok?' asked Anna, answering on the second ring being sat right by the phone in the lounge.

'I think so, I'm just having a bit of a panic,' and told her what was going on.

'Just pretend you're playing for me in the music room. I promise you, you are so good and even if you go wrong, I would bet that no-one will even notice. I'm going to stay up until you phone us back to let us know how it went. Go for it Connor dear,' and they quickly said their goodbyes.

Taking a deep breath, he went to be introduced to the band and tune the guitar. But he needn't have worried. Knowing their set so well, as they'd played at the pub so many times before, he'd actually been practising many of their songs at home, so knew most of them by heart.

As people stood up madly clapping and whistling at the end of the last song, he was handed a beer. Putting their instruments on the floor, they each took hold of their bottle.

'Cheers!'

'Cheers!'

'Fancy doing this again Connor?'

'Maybe.'

'Oi – you're not poaching my bloody bar staff Josh!' shouted Dave. 'Only joking! Connor if you want to do it, who am I to step in the way. You're too good for that!'

'Well, if you're stuck again, you know where I am,' said Connor, putting the guitar away while finishing his drink.

A month later, there was a local bands night at a town hall, and an emergency phone call had led to Connor joining them again. Watching other bands perform backstage before it was their turn; he turned to find Jack standing beside him.

'Oh hi Jack, you playing here tonight?'

'Yes, think we're on just after you!'

'So how's things... haven't seen you since school?' he asked Jack quietly.

'Yeah, not bad. We split up as a band after leaving school, so I've just found this band to play with for now. It's only the third time I've played with them, so still finding it pretty nerve-wracking to be honest.'

'Same here. I'm just helping this lot out as their bass player can't make it.'

'So what do you do otherwise?' asked Jack.

'Bit of bar work, bit of busking – how about you?'

'Similar, well the busking bit. I'm working shifts in Tesco just to earn some money.'

'Maybe we'll have to go busking together sometime?' suggested Connor.

'I'd like that,' replied Jack, just as Connor's band was announced as the next act to take to the stage.

'Catch you later, let's have a beer after!' said Connor.

'Great, see you later!'

*The Note That Changed Everything*

Jack and Connor have now made quite a name for themselves, building up a loyal, local following. Busking sessions, when they can fit them in around work, have proved to be pretty lucrative drawing large crowds, with shops now contacting them to play on their street to improve footfall. They have recently begun writing some of their own music, and a lad called Charlie has just joined them on vocals – Jack decided he would be much happier just playing lead guitar. They occasionally get to play at Connor's pub and a local radio station has just booked them a slot to play live in the next month.

And in Maida Vale everything is working out well. Anna is needing more help nowadays, with her years really catching up with her, but with Mandy and Connor on hand she is never on her own, or lonely. Chris and his family regularly visit and spend many evenings with them all - they have become great friends.

Standing at the sink in the kitchen, Mandy often looks out at the vast back garden and thinks of how things could have been. A smile and a shudder spreads over her body, the relief that life has worked out better than she would ever have imagined and how much she loves spending her days with Anna.

She and Anna have just had the most wonderful evening sat in the music room with a glass of wine, enjoying a performance from Connor, Jack and Charlie.

Putting away most of her earnings each month, Mandy knows that one day they'll have to move on - but the difference is *this* time they'll get to choose where.

*The Note That Changed Everything*

Three days ago Connor had a surprise visitor at work. Looking up, a big grin instantly appeared on his face. 'Sir!'

'Hi Connor, good to see you. A pint of ale please!'

'Oh, this one is on me.'

'I saw you play the other night and had to track you down, just to say how proud I am of you – cheers Connor,' and Mr Watson raised his glass.

# Do I Know You?

## Do I Know You?

Standing at the bar waiting to get the next round of drinks in, Melissa rummaged through her bag to dig out her phone that was ringing.

'Hello Melissa.'

'Er hi, who is this?' she asked, seeing the words 'private number' on the screen.

'How are you?'

'Er fine, sorry who is this?'

'I like the way you've done your hair tonight - it really suits you...' and the line went dead.

Looking down at her phone, she was suddenly interrupted by the barman asking for her order. 'Oh yes, sorry. Four vodka and cokes please,' and stuffing the phone back into her bag, she got out her purse.

Arriving back at their table, she passed the girls their drinks and told them about her weird call. 'Did you recognise the voice?' asked Amy.

'No. Anyway, doesn't matter, cheers everyone!' and their glasses were all clinked together.

By the time Mark met up with them later, they were all pretty merry. Dragging him out onto the dance floor, Melissa wrapped her arms around him for his token one dance, before he led her back to their table. Finishing their last drinks of the evening, Amy mentioned the call.

'Could it be someone at work?' asked Mark, slightly concerned.

'Don't think so. But anyway, no harm done - I'm sure it's nothing, so let's all forget about it, eh?!'

Six weeks later and with no other contact, everyone *had* forgotten about it.

*Do I Know You?*

With the music blasting out, Melissa was busy prepping the dinner, when the phone rang. Quickly wiping her hands on the tea towel, she grabbed the phone, balancing it between her shoulder and chin.

'Hello Melissa.'

She shuddered. *Oh my god, how do you know my home phone number?*

'Who is this?'

'Just wanted to check you were ok, that's all.'

'Well don't bother!'

'Now, now – don't get shirty with me.'

She hung up. The phone rang four times before clicking onto answer machine.

'That wasn't a nice thing to do, I'm only being friendly aren't I? Just wanted to see how you are doing today. Anyway, I can see you're busy, better let you get back to your cooking...'

Dashing to the hob, she turned off the ring and ran to the door. Frantically looking around everywhere, she couldn't see anyone.

Rushing back in, she pressed 1471. 'Caller withheld number'.

Pouring herself a large glass of wine, she was relieved when five minutes later the door opened and Mark was home. Hearing about the call, he grabbed the car keys and they set off for the police station.

'Sorry love, there's not much we can do at this stage,' said the uninterested police officer. 'Maybe keep a log of the times he calls. Often it just fizzles out, especially if you don't answer.'

But it didn't.

Jamming the door open, Melissa reached down to pick up all the magazines that had landed on the doormat. 'Oh no...' she whispered, as all the porn images flicked past her eyes.

Throwing them down on the floor, she kicked them into the corner not wanting to touch them again and rushed to wash her hands.

Seeing her face as he arrived home, Mark shoved them in a bag and sped off back to the police station. Dumping them on the countertop, he demanded that something be done. Putting a pair of gloves on, the police officer took hold of them and as the first one fell open at the centre spread, they could then see that things were escalating - Melissa's photo had been cut out and stuck on the original face.

'Jesus Christ, you must be able to take DNA samples or something from it?!'

The police officer confirmed that they would be taking them as evidence and would obtain any relevant information they could from them - they would be in touch shortly. In the meantime, he suggested changing her mobile phone number and ignoring unknown numbers on the home phone. Officers, covering their part of the city, would occasionally drive past to see if they got lucky. But again Mark was told, 'Not to worry. Many of these types would never dream of actually approaching the person.'

The phone calls continued on the home phone, but were apparently made from various public phone boxes so couldn't be traced. Meanwhile, Melissa was beginning to feel more and more twitchy and panicky.

'Good afternoon, Williams and Stanley accountants, how can I help you?'

'By answering your phone, that would be a good start...'

'Why are you doing this? I'm happily married, not interested ok – just leave me alone.'

'I don't think you realise how lovely you are – I just can't stop thinking about you. You're much sexier than the girls in the magazine, don't you think?!'

'I've been to the police you know... they're looking for you.'

'Oh yeah? We'll see. Anyway, is that a new shampoo you're using – your hair smelt lovely on the Tube this morning!' and he hung up.

'Oh my god!' she gasped, flushed in the face, scrabbling to find her phone in her bag to call Mark.

'Right, I'm dropping you to work every day and picking you up, ok? Well, actually you don't have a choice,' he said, cuddling her as she burst into tears.

'Why is he doing this?'

'No idea. But if you always have someone with you, he'll have to move on to someone else, won't he?! Can you get someone else to answer the phone at work? For a short time, stop all calls from men being transferred to you, unless it's me of course. They can take their number and you can phone them back. It could help.' Luckily her work were only too happy to do this.

'Melissa, it's Mark on the line for you.'

'Hello Melissa...'

'Oh my god,' she said with her heart instantly racing. 'How do you know my husband's name?'

'I just do. By the way, you look gorgeous today in your blue suit. - it's definitely your colour,' and he hung up.

Nervously pacing while waiting for Mark, she always worried if he was late that something bad had happened. Apologising profusely and explaining that he had been delayed by a longer than expected phone call at work, he quickly began to reassure her that whilst the calls were worrying, nothing could actually happen to her while she was never on her own.

\* \* \*

*I didn't expect to find her so quickly – especially as I was already busy seeing to someone else. But jogging past me with her headphones on, I was able to join Melissa's run from a distance.*

*You see it's perfect now really... headphones on, music blasting out, in their own world, very unaware of what is actually going on around them. It was much harder years ago... had to be so much more careful.*

*And the invention of social media... pure genius. I get to know so much about you, your friends and family, photos to print off, even videos sometimes to download. Thank you Mr Zuckerberg!*

*Joining her gym, keeping my distance but eavesdropping on conversations between her and Mark when they met up at the bar for a drink after their workouts, I could tell they really did love each other.*

*Shame it won't last.*

\* \* \*

With Mark worried about how it was affecting her, he arrived home one evening with a surprise.

'You know I love you so much!' she said grabbing hold of him to hug him so tightly.

'We could do with a break and some time out, just me and you,' he replied, tucking the tickets to a week in Venice back into their paper wallet.

They had the most amazing break, like a second honeymoon.

Opening the double doors, and stepping out onto the balcony overlooking the water, she took a massive deep breath. She had always dreamt of this moment.

Spending the week wandering the streets and walkways, stopping at cafes for a drink and bite to eat, she felt so relaxed and a world away from the nervousness she was increasingly feeling at home. Always looking over her shoulder, panicking if she thought she'd heard something, waking in the night convinced she'd heard creaking and someone coming up the stairs. She couldn't even go jogging on her own anymore.

But Venice was the perfect reset and they both agreed over a couple bottles of wine, that if he was going to approach her he would probably have done it by now. 'Just a weirdo perv who has probably never even had a girlfriend, the saddo.'

\* \* \*

*The loved up couple in Venice.*

*The cringey comments...*

*'Well jel, you two could be in a magazine shoot! Catch up when you get back Xx'*

*'Gorgeous couple'*

*Like, like, like...*

*Well it turns out the timing was perfect for me too. I'm almost ready for you to join me. Rachel still thinks she is going to get a chance to leave, if she does everything I want. But she will be joining the others...*

\* \* \*

Dumping their cases down in the hall, they were both completely shattered. Not really wanting it to end, they had decided not to waste time sleeping on their last day and instead spent it eating, drinking and people watching. A bumpy plane journey back had allowed little sleep, so they were both eager to grab something to eat and then crash out.

They agreed to leave sorting through the post until the morning, it could wait.

Sat at the kitchen table still feeling bleary eyed, they took a few sips of their coffees before starting to sift through the mountain of post.

'Uh oh, the credit card bill...' said Melissa, slowly ripping open the envelope.

'I should be getting my bonus next month, so that'll help a bit,' said Mark smiling.

Piling up all the junk mail, ready for the recycling tub, a jiffy bag slipped out from a free garden centre magazine. 'Ooh, some free seeds or something,' she said, sliding her finger under the flap.

Pulling a black lacy bodysuit out of the bag, a piece of paper dropped on the floor. Picking it up, the colour in her face instantly drained as she read: *'Look forward to seeing you in this soon x'*. Quickly scanning the outside of the jiffy bag, it was blank – it had been hand-delivered.

'When is it going to stop?' she cried.

The police took the bodysuit as evidence, along with the note. But with no fingerprints or clues, and CCTV being so limited in their area, they were yet again at a loss to be able to really help.

\* \* \*

*'Yes mum, I'm just waiting for it to brew then I'll be up. Do you want Rich Tea or Morning Coffee biscuits?'*

*'Rich Tea please, love.'*

*My dear mum... I love her so much; she means the world to me. Losing her legs to gangrene and becoming bedbound was so hard for her, especially since dad had passed. But I kept my promise... to always be there for her. The nurses pop in mornings and evenings to keep her dignity, she doesn't want me doing her personal care. But otherwise, everything is working out ok.*

*She worries about me, not having a 'life of people my age, filled with partying and girlfriends.' But actually it's working out really well for me... I always said I'd sort myself out. And thanks to dad, it was much easier than I expected.*

*Handing her her cup of tea and biscuits, she grasped my hand. 'Fancy watching a programme with me... Countdown is on soon?'*

*'I'd love to. Just got to pop out to feed the birds and then I'll be straight back.'*

\* \* \*

Work agreed Melissa could take another two weeks off, unpaid, owing to the circumstances. She didn't want to leave Mark's side, panicking at every noise, her imagination running wild.

She tried desperately to believe what everyone was saying. 'He's just some pervy weirdo, they rarely have the courage to approach you.' But knowing he was watching her, '*even smelling her hair for god's sake*,' made her suspect everyone who happened to be in her path. Constantly jittery, looking around everywhere she went, hoping she might just recognise the person on the phone, but to no avail. Everyone was just strangers that she would happily say she had never seen before, let alone talk to. She knew all the shopkeepers well, so could discount them, even the ticket staff at the station.

But then suddenly all communication ceased. No phone calls, no messages, no mail. Maybe everyone was right after all.

\* \* \*

*Dear mum... taking a turn for the worse was most definitely not in the plan.*

*Can't believe it took them twelve hours to stabilise her, sepsis suspected. Leaving her in intensive care was so hard but I promised her I'd be straight back... I just needed to sort a couple of things at home and get her toiletries and nightie.*

*Rachel is becoming a pain in the arse. Clinging on to me, promising me the world. But mum is my priority for now so Melissa will have to wait a bit longer. When I get a gap, I will deal with Rachel... just keep her fed and watered for now so she behaves herself.*

\* \* \*

A whole month went past with nothing. The police phoned for an update, happy that as they had reassured her before, 'Chances are it was just some weirdo with a bit too much time on their hands... ignoring them is always the best policy, they'll soon stop.'

Mark had spent the past two weeks walking her into the office and arriving to pick her up, with Melissa not even popping out for fresh air at lunchtime. But it had worked. Her nerves had calmed, heart rate returned to normal, and with the sun shining she started to feel the panic lifting.

'Fancy popping out for a coffee at lunchtime?' asked Kate, one of her colleagues.

'Yes - you know, I would love that.'

Sat outside the cafe, with their paninis and coffees, the birds tweeting in the surrounding trees, she suddenly felt at ease. Giggling with Kate, listening to her relationship woes, they finished their lunch and wandered back to the office. Mark arrived later to be greeted by his 'old Melissa'.

'Let's go out for dinner... to celebrate you feeling better!' he announced, taking her by the arm as they left the office to go to the car.

Falling into bed later, both slightly worse for wear, they had the best sleep in ages.

\* \* \*

*With mum not ringing the bell, which dad had setup from the house to the shed, life for a short time has been strangely peaceful. I hadn't realised the effect the constant dashing between the shelter and the house had had on me. Dad had set up the system, to save mum walking the quarter of a mile to the bottom of the garden to find him. She always used to say 'he probably spends more time down there than in the blimmin house... god knows what he gets up to. But he always seems happy when he comes in, so that's good enough for me.'*

*And the setup I found down there, well, it was probably best that mum didn't have a clue. But it was very handy for Lucy - my first girl.*

*Gosh... seems like ages ago now.*

*Rachel has been with me the longest... but not by choice. They are starting to worry me about mum, so I'm spending most of my time at the hospital.*

\* \* \*

'Come on – it's a lovely evening,' Mark said, trying to persuade Melissa to go out for a jog. It was the last hesitancy she had, and one he insisted he help her with.

On a beautiful summer's evening, the park was filled with all manner of people: dog walkers, joggers, picnickers and people just wandering around the lake, enjoying the fresh air before returning home. Mark and Melissa jogged around at a leisurely pace, loving the sense of freedom and fresh air.

Arriving back home, they jumped in the shower together before grabbing something to eat.

'So how do you feel now?' Mark asked, handing her a glass of wine.

'Really good... thank you.'

It had been nearly three months since they'd last heard from him.

'You know, I feel like I can try and go to work tomorrow on the Tube... on my own.'

'You sure? You can always chat to me the whole time on the phone, if you want?'

'Sounds like a plan.'

Whispering into her phone, pretending there was something up with her ear, Melissa tried her best to relax. Looking around the Tube, she studied all the faces. 'No... just the usual commuters at this time of the morning.'

'Perfect,' replied Mark, carrying on then talking about what their plans were for the rest of the week. Before she knew it, she was at the door to the office and entered to see Kate smiling at her. Saying goodbye to Mark, she agreed to do the same on the way home.

The following week she didn't feel the need to be on the phone.

\* \* \*

*Rachel's turning out to be worse than Hannah. Bloody scratch marks everywhere for me to repair and she's starting to smell... which is totally unacceptable. She's had her warning.*

*What's that? I haven't got time for this.*

*'Jesus Christ, you stupid bitch, give me that!'*

*'Who's this in the photo, you crazy bastard?!'*

*How the hell did she find it? Was sure I'd locked everything away before I left... must be the worry about mum.*

*Luckily I keep my Chloroform and a cloth to hand, just in case. No, you are not going anywhere... time for a long sleep Rachel... there we are, quiet restored.*

*Oh no, I missed a call from the hospital.*

*'Yes, sorry there wasn't any signal where I was, I'm leaving right now.'*

*'We are very sorry. Your mum passed away about ten minutes ago. Please... do come and sit with her for as long as you want.'*

*I want to howl the place down. 'Stupid fucking Tube delays and stupid Rachel for making me late!' I would probably have been here in time if she hadn't thrown a complete wobbler.*

*Kissing her on the cheek and taking a seat next to her, I don't want to let go of her hand. 'Oh mum.'*

*Telling her all the things I had wanted to, it's then time to wander back to the Tube. I can't really believe it - mum had always been there, and when she needed me I had always looked after her.*

*Sitting on her bed at home, I can finally let the tears out. But I also feel very angry... especially with Rachel.*

*'I'd have probably made it in time, you stupid bitch...'*

*It didn't take long... it was starting to get so much quicker and easier. Practice makes perfect, as they say. She of course pleaded and I hadn't meant to get so angry... usually it's much more peaceful and they know so little about it.*

*Blindfolded, in the lingerie I had bought them, offering me anything I wanted. But I know from the past, that they will always leave and never want to come back... and I can't accept that. So I sink the knife into their heart, as I hold them tenderly from behind, until their gasps fizzle out and they slump in my arms.*

*But Rachel hadn't deserved it to be like that. I enjoyed for a short time what she could do for me, but being hysterical and hitting me that hard, trying to leave and then making me miss mum's passing... well, she got what she deserved... frantic and brutal.*

*Gosh, digging out some old photos starts triggering lots of memories.*

*Lucy, my first ever girlfriend. Telling mum all about her, I felt the happiest I had probably ever felt. But sadly the feeling, it turned out, wasn't mutual. She made some nasty comments about me to her friends and even worse about our house and my mum. It's not our fault the council have left our area to go to rat shit is it? We'd complained so many times, but nothing was ever done. Mum and dad insisted that we were not 'bloody well moving, we must just make the best of it.' Not an easy task, when our area makes Jaywick look upmarket! As people left, houses were boarded up. Our nice neighbours sadly passed away over the years, leaving the area vulnerable to people you really don't want as neighbours. So we kept ourselves to ourselves. Once dad did his back in, the back garden was left to nature. By the time I was old enough to give a monkey's about it, it was too daunting a task. You couldn't see the house from the bottom of the garden. But one major positive - nothing in the area works, including the odd CCTV camera. Haven't seen a police car in years.*

*Finding the old air-raid shelter under the floor in the shed, stashes of magazines that mum definitely wouldn't have approved of, and then dad's old oil barrels filled with an unknown liquid, had been my first clue to his hobbies. Taking the small one that had nothing else in it, I asked the local council to analyse the liquid contents, said I wasn't sure how it could be safely disposed of, until I knew what it was... very handy working in the waste collection business. Said I'd found it clearing one of the fly-tipping areas.*

*It was a mix of lye and water - and a quick Google search told me everything I needed to know... thanks dad. I had wondered why there was a lead from the barrel to a power supply, turns out it just needs heating to work quickly. Fishing out the bones from the other barrels, I crushed them ready to be scattered at my next clearance area. Travelling all over the country, clearing up the mountains of rubbish dumped often in secluded areas is very beneficial.*

*Rachel will be ready in two days for my next clearance contract in Berkshire. Then before I take a break, there is of course Melissa.*

*Dear Melissa must be thinking I have forgotten about her...*

*Luckily I thought ahead... ever the Boy Scout. Once they told me mum was seriously ill and they were very concerned, I placed her last online lingerie order. I knew if the worst happened they would freeze her bank account, just like when dad passed.*

*Think I'm going to take a well-deserved day off... going to take mum somewhere nice for her last trip, it's the least I can do. Then I'm really going to try and make a new start. It will be so different when I have Melissa with me...*

\* \* \*

Sitting in the sunshine outside the cafe, enjoying their lunch break from work, Melissa was excited to hear all about Kate's new boyfriend. She was such a lovely work friend and had been so supportive with all her worries, Melissa was so happy to hear she had finally found someone that could be 'the one!'

'We must go out the four of us sometime – if you want to of course,' Melissa suggested.

'I would love that... think Mark will like him too. I'll see what Charlie thinks. I'm trying to keep under wraps how I feel, don't want to scare him off. But I get the feeling he feels the same and just isn't saying anything.'

Two weeks later, Mark and Melissa were showering and getting ready for their night out with Kate and Charlie. 'Fancy a quick glass of something before we leave?' he called up the stairs.

'A gin and tonic would be lovely thanks,' Melissa replied.

Forty minutes later, their taxi was battling with all the traffic, trying to get them to the restaurant on time. Handing him a tip and thanking him for making such an effort to get them there via the back roads, they were greeted with a lovely smile and shown to the table where Kate and Charlie were sat waiting. Two bottles of wine later and it was like an evening with old friends. They all had so much in common and by the end of the evening, were arranging their next get-together. Sat in a wine bar, with their last drinks of the evening, they were also discussing how as pissed as they were, the kebab van was still probably not a good idea. But it wasn't long before they were swaying in the queue waiting for their orders.

Tucking into their doner kebabs, they wandered over to the taxi rank. As usual the queue was huge so it was another forty minutes before they were all saying their goodbyes and finally on their way home.

\* \* \*

*With Rachel and mum both gone, I've got a lot more time on my hands. Placing mum's ashes on the mantelpiece in the lounge, I talked to her about where she might want to be scattered. As a family we had never been abroad or even on a proper holiday. But once a year, they always made the effort in the long summer holidays, to take me for a day trip to the beach... and fish and chips was always on the menu. I absolutely loved it.*

*So that was it... decision made. Fish and chips, and then a cliff top walk to say goodbye one last time.*

*Mum has always been my priority, so I have just promised her we will do this before anything else happens. The weather forecast is completely shit, but maybe that doesn't matter - it wasn't always good in the summer back then either.*

*Looking at the calendar and the jobs I have lined up, Saturday is looking good. I've checked the chip shop is open and filled the car with petrol ready.*

*And before I know it, I'm lifting the urn off the mantelpiece and placing it carefully in my rucksack. I am suddenly filled with overwhelming sadness, I suddenly feel very alone in the world.*

*As I queue for my lunch, the rain has eased and just a gentle breeze remains.*

*Sat on the bench, with mum next to me, I begin eating my fish and chips while my mind is busy reliving memories... happy ones. Dad in his string vest stretched out on a striped deckchair, mum in her dress taking me down to jump the waves in the sea together, holding hands, giggling as we misjudge and both get completely drenched... good times. A seagull has just tried to nick a chip... whack! Stupid bloody bird. Quick look around, good... no-one was watching.*

*And now it's time. Walking slowly up the incline, I stand for the last time with my mum to say goodbye.*

*'Love you!' I say as I take the lid off and let her go. And that's it then... back to the car and the drive home. I realise on the way back, that I feel so sad because I actually hate being on my own. But it's ok – I've got a busy house clearance on Tuesday and then a few days off before a week's contract in another county... then it's time for me to make the final arrangements to be with Melissa.*

*She seems back to her old self now... carefree... even saw her go for a jog the other day on her own... timing has always been one of my strengths I would say. And the time is starting to feel so right.*

\* \* \*

'Before our takeaway arrives and the wine bottle is opened, I need to talk to you about something.'

'Oh god, that sounds ominous,' Melissa replied smiling but trying to work out Mark's expression.

'I think you would agree that things are going brilliantly, yes?'

'Er, yes of course. Oh no, you're not going to tell me something bad are you?' she asked, starting to feel a little worried.

''Course not. No, I just wondered if we should reconsider the *'let's wait for at least five years before we think about having children, have some fun first,'* idea and bring it forward. Me and you are so strong and I love you more than anything in the world, I would love us to start a family sooner rather than later. What do you think?'

With teary eyes, she didn't really need to answer. 'I'd love that too,' she answered, hugging him with her arms held tightly around his neck.

A loud knock at the door, announcing the takeaway had arrived, suddenly interrupted the moment but it didn't matter – both excited at their change in plans.

A week later, she ditched her contraceptive pills and swapped them for folic acid tablets.

'Don't say anything to anyone though, will you – I don't want the pressure of mum asking all the time if we have any news yet?'

'I was going to say the same to you, we'll announce our news when it happens. Just need to think of an excuse if people ask why you aren't drinking much nowadays,' said Mark smiling at her.

'Oh heck... yeah, that's a sure giveaway. Have to think of something convincing,' she replied. 'But for now, let's arrange to meet up with Kate and Charlie and have a night out. It might be one of our last drunken ones for a while - you never know.'

\* \* \*

*She's looking so lovely tonight... a different twinkle in her eye. Standing near her at the bar, Mark has his arm around her waist and she is finding whatever he is saying in her ear, very funny. And then I hear the bombshell... she's getting rat-arsed on her last big night out before trying for a baby.*

*I watch them all evening, so in love. But she hasn't met me yet, or not that she remembers.*

*Think I've scrubbed up pretty well tonight myself, blending in with everyone, everyone unaware - just people watching. A nice looking girl has just had a quick chat at the bar whilst getting her drink, but I haven't got time for anyone else so leave it there.*

*Getting back home late, I'm starting to feel a bit angry now. I like to decide when I'm ready. But their news means I've got to act quicker than I had planned... I can't risk her carrying his child.*

*For fuck's sake! I've just noticed how much work I have on in the next three weeks, I'm going to have to make time now - probably the only chance. Luckily she is jogging on her own again now... and I know her route very well.*

\* \* \*

'Want me to come with you?' Mark called up the stairs, seeing the note that she had left if she had already gone.

'No, it's ok thanks. I'll only be about half an hour – you get changed and chill for a bit, before we decide what to have for dinner!' she replied, appearing on the stairs in her running gear.

Giving her a quick kiss goodbye, Mark then went upstairs after hearing the door click shut.

Selecting her playlist and popping one of the earbuds in her ear, she took a deep breath and smiled, setting off for the lake. Feeling such contentment in her life now, and excitement of their imminent baby plans, she had already calculated her best time to conceive this month so was hoping Mark wasn't feeling too tired. *'Maybe they should get a takeaway tonight – save cooking and washing up,'* she was thinking as she reached the first bench by the lake.

Whilst the weather wasn't great, with dark clouds looming ominously overhead, it was particularly quiet. Having a little chat to herself about not being silly, keeping one earbud out so she could hear everything around her, she sped up as she reached the most secluded part of her run. Heading through the avenue of trees, she was suddenly startled by a loud, gasping sound. Immediately scanning around her, she spotted a man collapsed on the floor just off the path. 'Oh my god, are you ok? Can't you breathe?' she exclaimed, rushing up to him.

Shaking his head, still gasping, he frantically pointed towards a large wheelie bin. 'What?' she asked, running over to it. Looking all around, she spotted a grey inhaler lying on the ground. Picking it up, she ran back to him, 'Is this yours?' she asked, passing it to him.

Eight puffs later, his breathing started calming and his pallor started to return.

'Thank you,' he whispered hoarsely, still taking deep breaths.

'You're welcome. Thank god I was here eh! Are you ok now? I really need to get going.'

'Could you just help me up? I think I dropped my phone in the panic – somewhere near my inhaler. Could do with phoning my other half,' he whispered, still gasping slightly.

'Of course.' But as she helped him up and started walking with her arm in his to support him, she suddenly started getting a bad feeling.

Seeing his mobile on the floor, she bent down to pick it up, just as a sudden strong chemical smell clamped around her nose and mouth.

'Hello Melissa...' and everything went black.

\* \* \*

*Quickly lifting her into the wheelie bin, at least no-one is around to say 'Can I just put this in your bin?' and handing me a stinking bag of dog shit! No, Melissa will not be joined by that.*

*Pressing the button, the bin rises up into the back of the van and we are nearly ready to leave.*

*'Shit!' her phone is ringing again. Jumping up and fishing it out of her pocket, I can see it's Mark calling. Running over to the edge of the lake, I throw it as far as I can. 'Plop' and it's gone.*

*Driving to the entrance, I suddenly have to swerve as a car screeches around the corner. I hear the words 'Sorry!' and a hand going up to apologise. 'Christ, it's Mark.'*

*Speeding down the slip road now to join the dual carriageway, I can at last start to relax. All this time I have thought about this... about Melissa. And she's with me now.*

*Everything is set up ready... can't believe how well this has gone... so easy too.*

*Clicking the radio on, switching channels to find some decent music, I'm hoping she will be a keeper - Melissa. Seven has always been my lucky number. Just need to keep making sure no-one gets suspicious, giving me enough time to convince her that she wants to be with me too.*

*Having watched her and Mark for a while now, I know what she likes too. The fridge is filled with lots of her favourite food... might even allow us to share the odd bottle of wine. You see Melissa is different... always has been. The others I didn't really develop feelings for, they were just building up my skills and experience for Melissa... don't want to disappoint her.*

*'Oh for Christ's sake! What the hell is going on up ahead?' Straining my neck to see, it looks like a car park - must have been an accident or something. Still, I made sure to gag her and tie her hands together, just in case it took longer than expected and she started to come around. Turn the music up, just in case she tries to make any noises.*

*Half an hour and we've only moved about two metres... starting to piss me off now but I mustn't panic. I can see our turn in the distance - it's only about quarter of a mile before we are off on our road, 'home and dry.' Trying desperately hard to be patient, I sing along to the next song.*

*Traffic news report has just interrupted the song. 'Serious accident causing long tailbacks and traffic is now queuing for more than two hours. Air ambulance is at the scene and the police are saying they hope to reopen the road in the next hour.' Oh my god, I think I just heard a banging noise coming from the back.*

*Properly panicking now, we need to go. If I quickly pull out onto the hard shoulder, I can drive down to our turning and get us home.*

*BANG!*

\* \* \*

In the panic, he hadn't noticed an HGV with mechanical failure, hurtling over the brow of the hill in the hard shoulder, desperately trying to come to a stop before hitting anyone. Ploughing into the side of his van, it then swerved into the barrier causing three other cars to join the crash.

Mobile phones started frantically dialling '999' and people rushed out of their cars to help the injured.

'Can you hear me mate?' said a young man, trying to see if there was any sign of life. Pressing his fingers to his neck, he could feel a pulse. Shouting to the paramedics, they sped over with the fire crew to the mangled wreckage of the van. Whilst he had a pulse, they could also see that his injuries were life changing.

'Have you checked whether there was anyone else in the vehicle?' asked one of the crew.

'Doesn't appear to be. Just a bin in the back, that miraculously is still in one piece.'

'You'd better check there isn't anything inflammable in it – that's all we need.'

'Jesus Christ!' the fireman called out, opening the lid to find Melissa. Removing the gag and snipping the ties, he carefully lifted her out and ran with her in his arms over to one of the ambulance crews. Having been surrounded by blankets, to make the bin more soundproofed, had been her 'saving grace.'

Ten minutes later, she opened her eyes to see a young lady wiping her cheek.

'Melissa... you're ok. You're safe,' she whispered to her.

'Mark... where's Mark?' Melissa managed to croak.

'He's on his way to the hospital, he's going to meet us there,' she answered, as they pulled out of the jam and headed to the hospital. 'Luckily, a local man named Charlie was only about six cars behind you and recognised you.'

'What about him? The man that took me.'

*Do I Know You?*

'Oh you won't need to worry about him anymore. He's in a really bad way. Between you and me, I'm not sure that he's going to make it, but don't tell anyone I said that,' she answered, smiling reassuringly at her and holding her hand for the whole journey.

Within five minutes of being checked over in the cubicle, the curtain was whipped back and Mark was there at her side. Tears filling his eyes, he leant over and kissed her. The nurse reassured him that she was absolutely fine, just some marks where the ties had started to dig in and the odd bruise from the crash.

The policeman waiting outside to talk to her was then given the ok to see her.

'Did you know him? Can you think of anywhere you may have seen him before?'

'No... I've been racking my brain, but really can't remember ever seeing him before?'

'All the contact he made with you before now makes us think he must have met you before in some capacity. Anyway, that's for us to work out. The important thing is that you get all the help you need to get over this – we have support ready in place to help you. And you can rest assured he definitely will not be in touch with you again.'

'Did he survive the crash?'

'For now, yes. I can't say too much, but he is in theatre and they are saying he only has a twenty-five percent chance of surviving the operation.'

Later that evening, she insisted she was ok to go home. The porter wheeled her out to Mark waiting in the car. Clicking in her seatbelt, he grasped hold of her hand, only letting go to change gear.

Searching his house, they soon came across the bell. Following the string, they battled their way through the 'jungle' of a garden, with nettles and weeds as tall as most of them, before arriving at the shed. Looking around, they soon found the hidden entrance to the shelter below and headed down the stone steps, grabbing the key off the hook at the bottom.

'Jesus Christ! Those poor girls...' gasped one of the officers, as he opened a locked door to find a wall covered in photos. Each girl taken, had their own section. Scantily clad pictures in very provocative poses, obviously taken from another location, together with Polaroids of them taken in the shelter. All pinned up like a soft porn parade. But *they* were nowhere to be found.

'What the hell is this in here?' shouted one of the officers, as he entered a small room at the back, with two old oil barrels and a gas mask hung on the wall.

'Don't open it!' another officer shouted, appearing at the door. 'Who knows what the bloody hell is in there! But the fact that there's a gas mask, it's not going to be good is it?!'

Wandering back into the room, a drawer was unlocked and a jewellery box pulled out and placed on the table. Opening the box, the contents confirmed their fears – each section contained the jewellery of one of the girls on the board, the necklaces and rings all matching the ones they were wearing in the photos.

Leaving forensics at the scene, they headed back to the station to start working on the identification of the girls and how they could possibly be linked.

They were also waiting on a call from the hospital to see how their suspect was doing.

Six hours later and the hospital were on the phone. The consultant confirmed that whilst he was still alive, they had had to amputate both his legs and he was also paralysed from the neck down. He was still unconscious and the next forty-eight hours would be critical.

Analysing all his phone and computer files, they found their link.

All the girls were unknown to each other and from all over the UK. But what most had in common were their own accounts on an adult subscription website, with direct messages and requests offering a very personal pay-per-view service. His bank records confirmed the monthly and on-demand payments he had made over the years; all under a different account name - the girls had no idea who they were really communicating with.

Lucy was the only one who had actually been his girlfriend. Going back in her online history, they found she had made some very unpleasant comments about him. A year later, she had never returned from a night out with friends.

Melissa, it turned out, had kissed him on the cheek once at primary school and was the only girl to ever show him any true kindness, sticking up for him with the bullies at school. Something she had long forgotten, but he hadn't. His search history showed he had even been looking at wedding venues and made some enquiries... 'for a Mr Alan and Mrs Melissa Roberts.'

Forensics confirmed the barrels had been filled with water and lye, an acid strong enough to dissolve virtually anything.

Carefully documenting all the company paperwork found for his clearance and fly-tip contracts, they then began mapping out a timeline of when the girls were last seen. Making links to the areas he had been working and the girls' disappearances, they even visited some of the fly-tip sites to see if any remains could be found. Sadly for the families, the areas were impossible to search fully and forensic officers believed that with only bones surviving the lye and water, they had probably been crushed and scattered.

Two months later, a court judge was now deciding his fate.

Unable to talk or move unaided, and being fed through a tube into his stomach, his future was looking very uncertain. Prison wouldn't be able to accommodate his complex medical needs, so the only option looked to be a psychiatric hospital.

So a month later, and finally able to leave hospital care, he was being wheeled into his new home.

As they passed one of the therapy rooms, one of the residents decided to introduce himself, whacking him around the head before he could be restrained.

Seeing the look of horror in his eyes, the porter smiled, 'Don't worry about Carl... he's just doesn't realise his own strength sometimes. We always get there as quickly as we can. Ian on the other hand, he can be a complete nightmare! Bit like you really, I guess.'

With only the squeak of his wheelchair breaking the silence, they then continued down the long, white corridor to what would end up being his final home.

www.ingramcontent.com/pod-product-compliance
Lightning Source LLC
Chambersburg PA
CBHW030321080526
44584CB00012B/655